How We Did It

How We Did It

THE SUBBAN
PLAN FOR

SUCCESS
IN HOCKEY

SCHOOL
AND LIFE

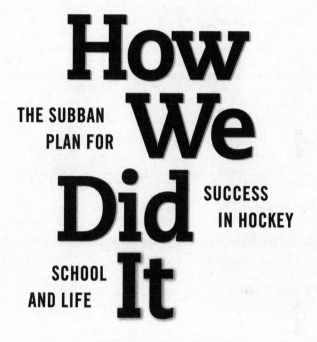

Karl Subban

and Scott Colby

RANDOM HOUSE CANADA

PUBLISHED BY RANDOM HOUSE CANADA

Copyright © 2017 Karl Subban

Published in 2017 by Random House Canada, a division of Penguin Random House Canada Limited. Distributed in Canada and the United States of America by Penguin Random House Canada Limited, Toronto.

www.penguinrandomhouse.ca

Library and Archives Canada Cataloguing in Publication

Subban, Karl, author
    How we did it : the Subban plan for success in hockey, school and life / Karl Subban and Scott Colby.

Issued in print and electronic formats.

ISBN 978-0-345-81671-9
eBook ISBN 978-0-345-81673-3

    1. Subban, Karl. 2. Hockey coaches—Canada—Biography.
3. Educators—Canada—Biography. 4. Fathers—Canada—Biography.
5. Success. 6. Parenting. 7. Autobiographies. I. Colby, Scott, author II. Title.

GV848.5.S83A3 2017   796.962092   C2017-901238-X

Cover and text design by Lisa Jager
Cover photo © Shayne Laverdière

Image credits:
Illustrations of the Subban family: REBL HOUSE Inc. & Laurine Jousserand
All uncredited images courtesy of Karl Subban
Printed and bound in the United States of America

10 9 8 7 6 5 4 3 2 1

Penguin
Random House
RANDOM HOUSE CANADA

This book is dedicated to my wife, Maria, and to our children,
Nastassia, Natasha, P.K., Malcolm and Jordan,
and to my many grandchildren

CONTENTS

How
We
Did
It

How We Did It

It's a Sunday evening in April 2015, and I am aware of how happy I am to be a hockey dad at this particular moment. My wife, Maria, and I are in the stands watching our sons play a professional hockey playoff game. On this night, my oldest son, Pernell Karl, better known as P.K., and his team, the Montreal Canadiens, are in a tough Game 6 battle with the desperate Ottawa Senators. The Canadiens are up three games to two in the first-round series and are eager to eliminate the Senators tonight.

But Maria and I are not with the 20,500 fans at the Canadian Tire Centre in Ottawa, watching P.K. play defence for the Habs.

Instead, we are closely following the game on the radio, using my iPhone. Maria and I share earbuds as we sit in the stands of the Dunkin' Donuts Center in Providence, Rhode Island. There, we are among the 5,289 fans watching our second son, Malcolm, play goal in a tense Calder Cup playoff match for the Providence Bruins, the American Hockey League (AHL) farm team of the Boston Bruins. It's Game 3 of the first-round series against the Hartford Wolf Pack, but it's Malcolm's first start of the playoffs.

Being emotionally present at two games at once: I have had the opportunity to live this moment many times. Win or lose, I love these occasions. But this night, my nerves are getting the best of me. I'm sitting on the edge of my seat, talking to myself. If someone happened to overhear me, they'd probably wonder what my problem is, since my commentary does not always match the action on the ice. How could they know my focus is on two professional hockey games and two sons in two different countries? I don't know what I would have done if our youngest son, Jordan, a defenceman with the Belleville Bulls of the Ontario Hockey League (OHL), had also been playing.

That night turned out to be a great one for Team Subban. Malcolm turned away forty-six of forty-seven shots, and Providence beat Hartford in a triple-overtime thriller. It was the longest playoff game in the P-Bruins history, and they took a 2–1 lead in the series. Back in Ottawa, P.K. registered an assist as the Canadiens beat the Senators 2–0 to advance to the second round of the Stanley Cup playoffs.

P.K. receiving an award from Walter Gretzky

No matter where you go in Canada, you will find hockey dads and hockey moms, those parents who drive their children to practices and games, at all times of day and in all kinds of weather; who coach and cheer and provide support. Walter Gretzky, the father of National Hockey League (NHL) legend Wayne Gretzky, is Canada's most famous hockey dad—the one who told his son not to skate to where the puck was but to where it was *going*. I wish all children could enjoy the support of a devoted parent, coach, teacher or mentor as they pursue their passions, whether on the field of play, in the classroom, on a stage, in a studio or in front of a computer. What is most important is to help children to find that thing they love to do and surround them with support so they can chase their dreams.

———

Long before I became a hockey dad, my dream was to be a hockey player. Specifically, I wanted to be Ken Dryden of the Montreal Canadiens. Ken Dryden and I had something in common: we were both goaltenders. As a child growing up in Jamaica, I'd played goalie in soccer. My family moved to Sudbury, Ontario, when I was twelve years old, and whether I was playing street hockey, or shinny on the ice rink near our apartment on Peter Street, goalie was my position here too. When I started watching the Canadiens on the local French-language channel, I looked for the player I wanted to be. Ken Dryden came up with Montreal in 1970–71, which made it easy for me to identify with him when I moved here. It also helped that he was good.

As the other kids and I played, we tried to emulate our role models in the NHL, and we wanted everyone to know who we were. I ceased to be Karl Subban in net—I was Ken Dryden. I even imitated his famous pose, standing tall in front of the net, leaning on his goal stick, which was angled to its maximum height, his glove hand resting on his blocker. He seemed to be saying, "I'm waiting for you."

Ken Dryden helped me make the transition to my new life. As a youngster and a new immigrant, I wanted to make friends. I wanted to feel like I belonged. Being Ken Dryden made it easier to fit in. I was no longer Karl Subban, the kid from Jamaica; I was Karl Subban, the kid now living in Canada.

Hockey was more than an idle pastime. When I wasn't watching the Montreal Canadiens on the French channel, or watching the Sudbury Wolves of the Ontario Hockey League in the Sudbury Arena, or listening to the Wolves games on CKSO radio with Joe Bowen doing the play-by-play, I was playing shinny. Once we made up our teams for games on the ice, or on the street, the competitive juices flowed with the drop of the puck or the ball. Win or lose, we had fun.

On one hand, I had a growing passion for the game. On the other hand, I was having difficulty accepting the fact that I couldn't play hockey on a real team since my family simply could not afford the equipment, the registration fees and the travel. I had this burning desire to play more and to achieve more, but my dream of being Ken Dryden had almost no shelf life. It wasn't too long before I realized I would have to park my dream in my dream chest with the hope that someday it would be resurrected.

As a young man, before I became a dad myself, I discovered another thing I loved to do, something that would become my life's passion, and that is helping children succeed. That passion took shape as I was pursuing a dream of playing in the National Basketball Association (NBA). I was drawn to basketball in high school when I reached six foot three, and I played collegiate basketball at Lakehead University in Thunder Bay, Ontario. The L.U. Nor'Westers, as they were called then, were often a Top 10 team in Canada when I played there in the late 1970s and early 1980s. During the summers, I coached kids at the Abitibi-Price basketball camps that Lakehead hosted. It was at these camps that I realized how much I enjoyed working with kids. Suddenly, another dream—to become a teacher—started to grow.

Now the National Basketball Association had a rival for my ambition, which turned out to be a good thing, as it became clear during my time in Thunder Bay that the NBA was not likely to be knocking on my door. After graduation, I enrolled in teacher's college at Lakehead and followed my new passion.

I was determined to become the best teacher I could, which led me to Toronto and a thirty-year career as a teacher and administrator, often in Toronto's toughest neighbourhoods. Those schools were where I felt I belonged, where I thought I could make the biggest impact, where I could be a difference maker.

As a Toronto public school principal, I would often give a room of students a simple proposition: "Anyone who wants to be better, raise your hand." Every hand shot up. That should come as no surprise—every child wants to be better. The problem is too many don't believe they can be.

There is a crisis today among our children. I saw it in the Toronto schools where I worked, and I see it today at the hockey arenas and in the playgrounds and on the streets and in the shopping malls. Too many children are adrift, too many children lack the direction and love and the support they need to be better. For these children there is no adult, or not enough adults, willing to step in, step up and lead the way till those children can find their own way.

Providing direction and support every day was the approach Maria and I took with our five children, each one of whom we are extremely proud of today. Our two oldest daughters, Nastassia and Natasha, are both teachers with the Toronto District School Board. Nastassia, who we call Taz, had an outstanding university basketball career at York University, and Natasha has excelled as a professional visual artist. All of our three sons, P.K., Malcolm and Jordan, have been drafted and signed by NHL teams. P.K., one the league's top defencemen, began his career with the Montreal Canadiens and is now playing for the

Nashville Predators, who made it all the way to the Stanley Cup finals in 2017. Malcolm was drafted in the first round by the Boston Bruins and plays in Providence in the AHL, and Jordan was drafted by the Vancouver Canucks and currently plays with its AHL farm team in Utica, New York.

Although I never got to play organized, competitive hockey, my passion for the sport never wavered. In fact, it has continued to grow through my children. In hockey, they have found something they love to do. The game became a window for them, and us, to see who they are and learn what they are made of. What gives me great satisfaction is that they are able to achieve something that was too far from my reach. The hockey door was never open for me—it was locked, with no key to be found. It wasn't till Maria and I had children that the door opened.

I believe it's important for parents, teachers and coaches to have dreams for our children, students and players. It is okay for your children to live your dream if it becomes *their* dream. When they're young, we may want the dream we have for them more than they want it. This is how it starts: you dream for them and they either take it or they go on to find their own dream. For them to achieve the dream, however, they must eventually want it more than you.

A career in hockey—making it to the NHL—is a dream shared by thousands of families, in countries around the world. I have met many of these families in the countless hours I have spent in hockey arenas across the land. Through the years, I have been asked one question over and over again: "Karl, how did you do it?" I call it the million-dollar question because if I were given a dollar for each time the question was asked, I would be a rich man today.

How do you explain how some people are able to defy the odds and achieve in life? It comes down to what you value, to the dreams you have, the choices you make. I like to say when most people come to a fork in the road, they see two options: go left or go right. What they don't see is that there's a third option: go straight ahead and make a new road.

The same year I came to Canada, Maria and her family moved from the Caribbean island of Montserrat to Toronto. Subban is not a common hockey name. Jamaica and Montserrat are known for their sunshine, beaches and rich cultures—but hockey? Not on the radar. Our families came to Canada for jobs and education, for opportunities. Maria and I saw ice hockey as one of those opportunities, allowing our boys to embrace a sport that so many Canadian children and families enjoy playing, watching and following.

When I met Maria I was happy to discover she was a hockey fan as well. She cheered for the Toronto Maple Leafs; I was a die-hard for the Canadiens. Our children all knew the *Hockey Night in Canada* theme music before they could walk. When Toronto and Montreal played, the noise in our house was louder than the cheering inside the Montreal Forum or Maple Leaf Gardens.

Ice-skating was something we did as a family. Taz and Tasha learned how to skate before the boys and even helped me teach them—you could say it was an extra-early start to their future careers in education. The boys were on the ice when they were in diapers, and skating and hockey became part of who they were. For our three sons, it was their dream that became their identity—not their last name or where their parents were from.

This is what I mean about creating that third path: it's about breaking stereotypes. So when people ask me why we had our boys play hockey, I want to ask them, "Why not?" No one will ask a family from Red Deer, Alberta, why they have their kids playing hockey. They just do it. That is what Canadians do. We just did it. We loved the game. We enjoyed watching hockey and we knew our children would love playing it too. And maybe one day they would be wearing a Leafs jersey or a Habs jersey, playing on a Saturday night, giving Mom and Dad the chance to cheer even louder.

What was it the boys possessed to allow them to succeed, to become professional hockey players, to achieve a dream thousands of hockey-playing children aspire to but only a small percentage will realize? The answer comes down to one word. It is the same word for our sons, and our daughters, and every person on the planet: potential.

Whether it was our five children, or the thousands of kids I taught or coached, or the school board staff I worked with, or my grandchildren today, I see everyone the same way; I see each person carrying a gift inside them that they are born with, and that gift is their potential. It has been my job as a father, as a principal and as a leader to develop that potential. And I deliberately don't say "reach" that potential because I don't believe a person ever reaches their true potential. That is something you should always be striving for, no matter how old you are.

Maria and I saw our children's potential from an early age. Many people think our sons are natural-born hockey players. It's true they are gifted, but so is everyone else. Each person is born with the same gift. I honestly believe that. Where that gift takes you, I don't know, but you are born with it.

That gift is something I like to call the GPS—the Growing Potential System.

Every child is born with a GPS that needs to be loaded. The earlier it can be loaded to go somewhere positive and do something good, the better off our children will be. You are born with potential, but you are not born with the skills and the talent. Those need to be developed over time. A barber is not born to be a barber. He needs to practise. An electrician is not born an electrician, but your child may have what it takes to become one. Wrapped up in your potential are the skills, the abilities, and the talent needed to overcome the barriers to becoming an electrician.

P.K. was born into an environment that loaded his GPS. It is important children know where they are going, and the earlier they know what they are good at, the better off they are going to be.

There was a time when P.K. expressed an interest in playing basketball. I don't know how good he would have been if he put in the same amount of time, effort and determination as he did with hockey. You just never know. I wouldn't say he couldn't have made it in basketball. That is the beauty of possessing the gift; you don't know where it is going to take you.

As an educator, I could never tell anyone that they shouldn't go after something because they might not succeed. That said, I always maintain that goals have to be attainable and relevant. P.K. had a more realistic chance of making the NHL than the NBA based on his height—he's six feet even—and based on being from Canada. We produce more hockey players than any other country in the world. We have the best minor hockey system in the world and the best league in the world with the Greater Toronto Hockey League (GTHL), and we have great coaches and an impressive system of support, from Hockey Canada on down. I'm not surprised kids from this country make it in hockey. Canadian kids are born with their skates on. I'm not surprised P.K. made it, or that Malcolm and Jordan are on their way; the ingredients are there to help kids make it. It's the perfect environment.

When I meet parents of high-achieving children, I often asked them the same question I am so often asked: What did you do to pave the way for your children's success and achievement? The answer usually involves the same ingredients: high parental involvement; a supportive and stimulating environment; a focus on excellence; the pursuit of a big goal or dream. This is a potent recipe for children to find success. It gives children a chance to make something of themselves. Children see opportunities when you set the table for them.

Maria and I followed the same recipe for raising our children. For example, we were involved in their day-to-day activities. If we were not there physically, we were with them in other ways. Like my parents did with me, Maria and I planted our voices in the back of our children's minds. When they needed directions, they turned up the volume on our voices, which reminded them of our expectations and reinforced them.

My own parents' expectations of me were made crystal clear, and I could always hear their voices in the back of my head saying, *Yes, Karl* or *No, Karl.* I didn't want to let them down. Their voices acted like stop signs or yield signs. They never wanted me to get into trouble, and I never wanted to embarrass them or let them down. As a child, you learn right from wrong over time, day by day. As a parent, that is what you do: teach them the stop signs and the yield signs. Even today, I can give my kids "that look," and they know exactly what I'm thinking.

My sons left home at sixteen, and thank God they never got into any major trouble. I know they took with them those voices that are stop signs: *Stop. You are drinking too much. Stop. You need to go home now; you have practice in the morning. Stop. You have a game tomorrow night.* I learned from my parents and my children learned from me what the word *no* meant. With child rearing, after a while, if you are still telling them "no" every time, good luck. Once they know what it means, you don't have to tell them over and over. A crucial step to achieving that goal—of getting children to know what "no" means—is for parents to spend time with their children. This demonstrates to them that you care. You can discipline your children all you want, but if they don't know you care, it doesn't matter. The art of disciplining is shaping the will without breaking the spirit.

Maria and I did not start out with a Team Subban recipe. There was no blueprint for raising our five children, and we never formally articulated one. Our recipe consisted of providing the basics—food, shelter, safety, love and lots of activities, such as outings to the park, helping with homework, making kites, cooking together. The goal of excelling in school sports, however, was stamped in the minds of our children from early on in their lives. Children want to please their parents, and when they work to please you, they are working to please themselves, making hard work its own reward. The demands and expectations you set for them offer some of the strongest evidence that you love and care about them.

Over time, however, a recipe based on my parenting and

teaching did emerge. Part of that recipe is loading your kids' GPS. Another ingredient is to remember that parents can't do it alone. You need help. Even your best is not good enough. There is an African proverb that says, "It takes a village to raise a child." That is true in North America today. As parents, you cannot do it alone. You need a team. As I like to say, the bigger the dream, the bigger the team. Team Subban did not do it alone. We had a lot of help along the way.

There is nothing easy about raising kids. There are distractions that steer children away from studying, such as partying, doing drugs, wasting away hours on the computer or on their phones with games and social media, where children are often bullied by their classmates and find their self-esteem attacked. So it is really important your children are engaged in something beneficial that they love to do. I like to call this activity the "extra parent." Every child can use an extra parent. It keeps your child focused; it keeps them on the right track and away from destructive temptations.

Maria and I have been identified as people who are "doing it right" as parents because of the successes our five children have had. I never get too caught up in any praise we may receive, nor do I want to believe my own press. I have a guiding thought in my mind that has always worked to keep me focused, real and grounded: just because our children are making it in their profession does not mean they are making it in life. I am happy for my children and their achievements in hockey and education, but the most important reward for me as a parent is for them to make it in life.

As I told P.K., "If you are not a good person, you will never accomplish your goal of being a good hockey player. If you are not a nice person, you are not going to be a happy person and you will not reach your potential." I'm inspired by the story of Brooklyn Dodgers manager Branch Rickey and his message to Jackie Robinson as Robinson was about to break Major League Baseball's colour barrier in 1947. He said: "Jackie, we've got no army. There's virtually nobody on our side. No owners, no umpires, very few newspapermen. And I'm afraid that many fans will be hostile. We'll be in a tough position. We can win only if we can convince the world that I'm doing this because you're a great ballplayer and a fine gentleman."

Some parents think there are shortcuts, that they can avoid the hard work, or that certain children are just naturally gifted, blessed with some sort of genetic inheritance. This misguided notion was perfectly illustrated one spring evening in 2011 when I walked into the Herb Carnegie Arena on Finch Avenue in North York for one of Jordan's Greater Toronto Hockey League playoff games. Jordan had just turned sixteen and was in his final year with the Toronto Marlboros. It was his draft year, and he was a Top 10 OHL prospect. These playoff games attracted many scouts. Every game counted. Every move on the ice was being evaluated. I was nervous, filled with anticipation and hope for a good game for Jordan and his teammates. As parents, we worry. That's what we do.

The arena was packed and buzzing. You could feel the energy. The fact the game was being played at Herb Carnegie Arena added to the flavour of the night. I always enjoyed when my sons played there, partly because of who it was named after. Carnegie, an outstanding black hockey player in the 1940s and 1950s, was

born in Toronto to Jamaican parents and should have been the
first black hockey player in the NHL. He never made it, due to
the colour of his skin. In his impressive autobiography, *A Fly in
a Pail of Milk*, Carnegie wrote that Toronto Maple Leafs owner
Conn Smythe once said he'd pay $10,000 to the man who could
turn Herb Carnegie white. Carnegie had a rough ride in hockey,
but he won many awards and titles playing semi-pro, mainly in
leagues in Ontario and Quebec, before becoming a champion
senior golfer after he retired from hockey in 1954. In 1955, he
established the first registered hockey training school in Canada
and later worked as a financial advisor for thirty-two years.

So it was fitting that Jordan was playing such an important
game at the Herb Carnegie Arena, a place where P.K., as a five-
year-old, had scored on an impressive double-deke move in a
shootout.

And there's another great thing about Herb Carnegie Arena:
without a doubt, it has the best arena popcorn in the Greater
Toronto Area. On this night, as usual, the intoxicating smell of
the popcorn was everywhere and acted as a powerful magnet,
pulling me to the snack bar. Anxiety covered me like a blanket,
and I was looking to eat something to calm my nerves.

I came to the game alone. With my popcorn in one hand
and a coffee in the other, I was heading to the stands when I
bumped into a hockey dad I had known for some time. This
acquaintance introduced me to a friend of his, a young hockey
dad in his late twenties. At least I assumed he was another dad.

The man promptly said to me, "I have a proposition for you."

Hmmm, okay. "What do you have in mind?" I asked. *I hope
he doesn't want me to train his kid*, I'm thinking. *I don't have time
for that.*

"I would like you to make a baby with my wife."

I was stunned. Before I could stammer out an answer, he offered to pay me.

Now I couldn't help but laugh, and after quickly doing some math joked, "Thirty-five years ago I would have done it for free."

But my smile quickly disappeared. *This poor guy thinks it's all in the genes,* I thought. He was clearly aware of Jordan's success; he knew of Malcolm, a top goalie prospect with the Belleville Bulls who had played on the national under-17 team; and P.K. was already making some noise in the NHL. This man saw me as having the right hockey genes and wanted a child who would be similarly blessed. But the fact is, of the twenty thousand to twenty-five thousand genes in our body, scientists have yet to identify any that predispose a person to becoming an elite hockey player.

Maria and I had five children, and we wanted them to have the highest level of success in school and life. I hoped this guy was joking, but he seemed to fit the archetype of the over-zealous hockey dad, always looking for an advantage or a shortcut. He wasn't interested in what Maria and I did to raise three elite hockey players. I'm sure he didn't even know about our two talented, successful daughters. But many other parents, teachers and coaches do want to know, and that is why I wrote this book. There is no such thing as a hockey gene, and I hope by telling my story I can show what it takes to raise strong, successful children; to teach them how to dream, how to be a little better today than they were yesterday and how to make their dreams a reality.

It Starts with a Dream

Your past is your history; it won't accurately predict your future, but it can certainly have an influence on it. It did on me, as an adult, as a father and as a teacher. I was born in Jamaica in 1958 and spent the first twelve years of my life there, in Portland Cottage, a small town roughly in the mid-point of the island on the southern coast, fifty kilometres southwest of the capital city of Kingston. It was a happy childhood of sun-drenched days filled with family, sports and great food. We didn't have a lot, but my parents, Sylvester and Fay, provided me and my three brothers— Hopeton, Patrick and Markel—with all we needed.

My dad was employed at the Monymusk sugar cane factory, where they made molasses, brown sugar and our famous
Jamaican rum. My mother stayed at home, but worked side
jobs sewing. Dad was a reliable employee and believed in doing
a good job. Despite working as a mechanic on diesel trucks, he
did not own a car. Our family car was my dad's bicycle, which
he rode to work: sixteen kilometres in the morning and sixteen
kilometres home in the evening, no matter how hot it was. And
it was always hot.

Dad would also take my brothers and me—I was the second oldest—to the beach with him on the bike on Saturdays
and Sundays. I have no idea how we all fit on that bike, but he
would ride us the five or six kilometres to the ocean. We'd play
in the ocean even though we never learned to swim. We'd grab
pieces of bamboo or tire tubes to float on. Or we'd try to ride
the waves like California surfers. The waves would crash on the
beach and we'd hold on to that bamboo for dear life. My mother
would stay home on those beach days, taking a well-deserved
break from her energetic sons.

Growing up, my brothers and I knew we were loved—we
never had a lot, but we always had enough of what we truly
needed. If something had been missing we would not have
known it; we were very happy. Our family cared for us and
loved us. They didn't have to say it in so many words—we just
knew it. We also knew showing respect was paramount. There
were four expectations placed on me, like a licence plate on a
car, and they came from my parents, my extended family and
the community. These expectations were as ubiquitous as the
hot Jamaican sun. They were always there in my conscious and
unconscious mind:

1. Work hard in school.
2. Behave well, watch your manners and always respect your elders.
3. Look clean and neat, especially outside the home.
4. Be good at something and make your family proud.

These expectations set the tone for the early years of my childhood and, much later, influenced the expectations I had for my own children.

When I think back to how my parents raised us, it's clear that education was important to them. They didn't go over-board pushing us—they never said I had to be a lawyer or a doctor or anything else. All we knew was that we had to attend school and do well. And since the school never had to call home, my parents assumed everything was great. They would always hear people say, "Oh, your boys are so nice." We were never in serious trouble—and maybe trouble never came across us. We saw that our parents were working hard, and we did not want to disappoint them. And whenever I needed money to play soccer, or go on sports trips, or buy running shoes, they were always supportive. And there were the little things that showed they cared, like the way my dad always made us our school lunches, even when we were in high school in Sudbury. He would print our names in upper-case letters on our lunch bags: Karl, Rex (Patrick's nickname) and Mark. Inside would be sandwiches, fruit and juice. His metal lunch bucket stood right beside our bags.

While my dad was a loving father, he also instilled disci-pline and set rules. We had to be home when he got home from work, for instance. I had an idea of what time my dad would

Sylvester and Fay Subban

be home. If I was next door, I knew when to start my lookout. I could see dad about a kilometre away, riding home on his bicycle. Before he got home I would already be there, my feet and face washed, my hair combed. Once dad was home, there was no leaving the yard—that was it. It may seem strict now, but that was their way of raising us. They didn't want us running all over the place, especially in the evening.

Corporal punishment was ingrained in our society. Dad was definitely the authority figure in our home, and he used corporal punishment when he felt it was necessary. I got his belt across my behind if I was fighting with my brothers, for instance, or if a neighbour or an elder came and complained to my parents about our behaviour. I was the oldest child at home at the time, and

I was held to higher expectations. (My older brother Hopeton was living with my grandparents.) The punishment was never so severe that it would break the skin or leave a bruise. Corporal punishment wasn't just at home, either; you also got it at school when you were late, or did something out of line.

But I must stress that for every ounce of punishment there was a pound of love. I was never afraid of my dad. He was always there for us; he provided for us and he gave us lots of love. As I grew older, I started to run from my dad when it came time to be punished. Who wants to be hit? By the time I was eight or nine, he could no longer catch me, and that was the end of it.

My parents' influence reached beyond the house too. When we were outside the home we had to be on our best behaviour. If our family was invited over to someone's house and I was offered a glass of water, I would look to my mom or dad to see if it was okay. That's the way it was—I knew the limits, and those boundaries were painted in red. My brothers and I were allowed to be boys, but we also had to know how to behave in public and to not bring shame on the family. You learned quickly in life that families had reputations. Subban, Peters and Bartley, the names of my immediate and extended family, were reputable names in the community, and we had to live up to them.

I believe that knowing boundaries is crucial. If you love your children, you discipline them. And by discipline I don't mean spanking—I mean teaching your children that there is a word called *no* and children should know what it means. My mom led by example, and although she tried to be a disciplinarian when we got into conflicts, she never followed through. Whereas all my dad had to do was look at us. My mom gave us an inch, but we knew it was a yardstick—the extendable kind. She was loving and caring, and I think she invented second chances.

Mom was industrious and creative and never had idle hands. When she wasn't cooking or cleaning, she was an excellent dressmaker and skilled at embroidery. There was no project that intimidated her. And she wasn't afraid of the hammer and the nails, either: when my parents built their house, she was the one who built the kitchen in the back.

My mom was also the one who taught us how to read and write. There is something about growing up in the West Indies at that time that you need to understand. Children were not allowed to look an adult in the eye when speaking to them. And that went double if you were being disciplined. "You're looking at me!" is how a child would be scolded. "You think you're a man? You think you're a big man?" It was intimidating. And even if you weren't being disciplined, you were discouraged from having conversations with adults. I believe this practice had the effect of holding us back. In teacher training, I learned that a child's vocabulary grows in three ways: by listening to adults speak, by speaking to adults and by reading. I notice that even today, kids who come from Jamaica will stand up when they have a question to ask but they won't look you in the eye. We know now that good listening involves looking someone in the eye, and if you haven't been taught that, the way you express yourself will suffer.

Reading did not come easily to me. I struggled with it. My mom did her best to teach me. We'd sit outside in the backyard late in the afternoon, before the sun went down, in the shade of the coconut trees on a bench or wooden box. We read simple picture books, such as *Fun with Dick and Jane*. There weren't a lot of books to be had—mostly, we'd read the *Daily Gleaner* newspaper. If you don't see yourself as a reader, it is very difficult to make it a positive experience. My mom did her best to help me, and looking back, I am so glad she tried.

Listening to the radio was another way I built my vocabulary. I loved listening to cricket, and of course music was an important part of our culture. Learning songs is a vocabulary builder, though I admit that my parents may not have liked all the vocabulary I learned from some of the songs.

Another vivid memory I have of Mom from that time is her sitting in the backyard sewing. This was not an unusual sight, but on this particular day she was making something for me on her Singer sewing machine, and I could barely stand the excitement. She laid out brand new khaki cloth she'd bought from the store, measuring it against a pattern she had drawn up and then carefully cutting the fabric before sewing a pair of pants, then a shirt. She was making a new school uniform for my first school trip. I was about seven or eight, and I had never left home before. Mom would be up all night working to make it look and fit just right. The end result was a bit loose for my liking but tailor-made to the expectations of my parents.

Our class went on a day trip to Dunn's River Falls near Ocho Rios and Port Royal, an old pirate colony that sank into the sea during an earthquake, and then to the zoo in Kingston. School trips were especially momentous because we didn't have a family car, so we never went anywhere, literally. There were no Sunday drives. My parents understood the value of the trip, so Dad worked overtime to pay for it. I probably had trouble sleeping for five days. We were sent off on the small bus with some corned beef and hard-dough bread to eat and a little spending money. The trip made a huge impression on me. We had heard of these places but obviously had never been. Dunn's River Falls is a major tourist attraction. We were awed by its beauty but not allowed to swim that day because we didn't have a change of clothes. The other memory I have of that trip was the iguana at the zoo. We had never seen these large, colourful lizards where we lived. It's funny which memories survive over the years.

A great benefit for my brothers and me was having my mom at home until I was twelve years old. It was during those years my mother taught me how to cook. One year, Mom had to have surgery and she couldn't move for a while, so she taught me how to make fried dumplings and chicken back. Dad was at work, and Patrick and Markel were too young to help at the time. Chicken back is mostly bone, but it was a delicacy that we loved. I still cook it the way Mom taught me. I cut off the fat, then season it. We used to use monosodium glutamate back then, and I added some thyme, onions and soy sauce and let it marinate. Then I sautéed it and cooked up some yams and green bananas. Mom, sitting in a chair, gave me step-by-step instructions. It was like having a live YouTube cooking video. Even when I was a grown adult, my mom remained a YouTube sensation for me. I'd call her if I needed help with something I was cooking. But I guess Mom shouldn't get all the credit; my dad cooked as well, and he's still a very good cook today. My brothers are too.

Cooking is one of the ways our parents spent time with us. Spending time with your children is so important. When he was young, P.K. once said to me, "Daddy, I've spent more time with you than anybody on Earth." I think I could have said the same thing to my parents. The ones you spend the most time with influence you the most.

In my case, it wasn't just my parents—my great-grandparents, grandparents, aunts and uncles all had a hand in raising me. They did not hesitate to tell you when you were good, or when you were not so well-behaved. One time I was not so good involved my Uncle Desmond, my mother's younger brother. He owned a scooter that, in my eyes, was like a Harley-Davidson motorcycle. He often worked on his prized possession in his yard. It seemed like it was always broken and he was always fixing it; he'd rev it up and pieces would fall off. He was a serious man who never wanted to see you laughing at him or his scooter. I'd ridden on the scooter, once, when Uncle Desmond was away. His brother, Uncle Owen, gave Patrick and me a ride on the back, but he wasn't supposed to be driving it. It had just rained and the potholes in the dirt road were filled with water. Uncle Owen lost control of the scooter while driving over a pothole. I jumped off and escaped injury, but Patrick went down with the bike. He still has a mark above his eye as a permanent reminder.

One day, when I was about seven or eight, my Uncle Desmond had, as usual, taken the bike apart, and the parts were scattered around. I snuck off with the light bulbs and sold them to buy myself a treat. Why would I do that? Well, I wasn't a perfect kid, and we all know kids can do stupid things.

Now, you need to understand, in our neighbourhood there were no secrets. If I gave someone a dozen mangoes from our mango tree, everybody would know—and they'd know that same day. My uncle found out I sold the parts. Somebody told me he was looking for me. I hid at my great-grandparents' place, but he eventually found me. Did I ever get a licking from my

Uncle Desmond that day! I don't remember how much I sold the bulbs for, but what I do remember is what my action cost me. And I learned an important lesson: sales was not a good profession for me.

Jamaica's motto is "Out of many, one people," and this phrase is how I explain the relationship with my extended family. It was wonderful growing up with them, and we are still close today. My family's reputation was built on a foundation of service to others, and that service revolved around the church. My maternal grandmother, Vashtie Peters, founded a Pentecostal church in my district that is still standing tall and going strong.

To make it in life you need many giving hands. When my parents started out, my grandparents were there for them, providing help for them to survive but also to thrive. Those values have stayed with me, that kindness and caring. My grandparents' fingerprints were all over the success and achievements of my parents, especially in those early years together. And my parents returned the favour after they moved to Canada, helping their parents. My parents were in their teens when they got married and started having children. They initially lived with different relatives but mostly with my mom's grandparents. Luckily, we all lived in the same area around Portland Cottage.

By working hard, my parents were able to save enough money to realize the dream of owning their first home. Back then in Jamaica, it was a tremendous achievement if you had enough money to buy land and build on it. There was a room in the front where we kept our beds and tables and clothes, and a kitchen at the back. There was no bathroom, just an outhouse. The house wasn't big, but it was big enough for us. I can imagine how proud my parents were to achieve what they did. They created one big, happy family in the small house they built. When I look back on it, those were great times, happy times. My dad, who now lives in Brampton, Ontario, with Markel and his family in the summer, spends his winters in Portland Cottage and still owns that house and rents it out. It sure doesn't look as big as it did when I was a child.

Besides providing us shelter and a safe place to sleep and eat, that small house also made our family close, both literally and figuratively. I think that closeness came from the way we were raised. You are sleeping in the same bed, eating off the same plate. That bound us together, and you'll never be able to separate us.

When I turned seven, I went to Portland Cottage Primary School, which was known as the Big School because it was for the big kids. The smaller students, what we would consider junior and senior kindergartners, went to what we called infant school. There was one main road, called School Road, that led in and out of my district. It was mostly dirt and snaked its way through our sprawling little town to the Big School, a one-storey cement-block building, painted off-white, that sat in the middle of about two hectares of land on the outskirts of town. I could walk there in about ten minutes, and along the way I'd pass by my grandfather and great-grandfather's house. My great-grandfather, George Bartley, owned a large parcel of land that bordered on the back of the school property. After he retired from Monymusk, he worked as a farmer. On my walk to school I passed through part of his property, which

My great-grandparents George
and Caroline Bartley

was populated with fruit trees and singing birds. The mango
trees, coconut trees and cashew trees lined my path to the
schoolyard. Picking mangoes and eating them was my favourite activity going to and from school.

I loved the Big School. I had many friends, and I got to play
cricket and soccer in the large field beside the school. We had a
lot of fun, but school was to be taken seriously. We had to be on
time, and when you were late, you would hear about it from the
teachers and you felt it from the principal, Mr. Grant. He was
always at the school entrance, waiting to meet late-arriving students with his long, flexible bamboo cane. We knew to form a
straight line with one hand extended, palm facing up. Each late
arrival received two or three lashes. It would hurt, but you could
never show you were hurting.

Inside, the school was one big room. Classrooms were created using chalkboards and furniture. As a student, you might
not have been able to see everything in the school, but you
certainly heard everything. Mr. Grant's desk was located at the

front on a wooden platform. He sat up there like a lifeguard, eyes scanning the two hundred students. You didn't have to go too far to visit him. It was public knowledge when he doled out discipline, which was not always good for self-esteem. Nobody needed social media to be shamed.

Recess and lunch break are universally the best times for students. Before the principal rang the bell to signal the start of lunch, I could smell the hot oil frying, cooking what my belly wanted. As the bell began to ring the learning stopped, and I was on the mark and ready to sprint to the kitchen located near the school's front entrance, to buy my lunch of fried dumpling with codfish fritters and ginger beer.

Before I made it to the kitchen, however, I often had to deal with my great-grandfather, who would frequently sit on a wooden box at the school's front gate, waiting for me. His machete was always parked close to him, taking a break from cutting, weeding and pruning his farm. The gremlins in my stomach had to wait for food on the days my great-grandfather saw me coming. When I was close, he would call me over to sit on his lap. That's when the tickling would start and the laughter would replace the hunger that had been my focus. He never called it tickling, however; he called it forking. He had long fingers that went along with his tall frame—he was well over six feet. He would tickle me until I ran out of laughter, and I guess he never got enough of it, because he was there a couple of days a week. This special time with my great-grandfather has stayed alive in my memory. He gave me two things: mangoes and his time. To me, they were both equally sweet.

———

When I wasn't in school, or sitting on my great-grandfather's lap, I was usually outside finding fun things go do. We didn't have a television in the house or even a phone. Our only luxuries were a radio and running water. But in Portland Cottage in the 1960s, there were many activities to keep us busy. We played marbles, flew kites, picked fruit and hunted crabs.

May was crab-hunting season, when the rain, lightning and thunder brought the crabs out of their holes. We'd get up early in the morning and head to the sea; a torch created out of a Red Stripe beer bottle—half filled with kerosene and with a rolled up newspaper for a wick—would light the way. I'd put on gloves to catch the crabs by hand, or else I'd use a long metal hook. The burlap bag on my back would be the home for my next meal. There were three ways of preparing the crabs: you could boil them with a little salt or with Scotch bonnet or bird peppers; you could cook them in curry; or you could make them my favourite way, formed into patties, which is how my mom made them.

As much fun as I had hunting crab and flying kites, there was one activity that would become my dream and my passion: playing cricket. I can still picture my dad dressed in white, ready to go to the cricket grounds, where he played on both his company team and the community team. I remember spending many hours at the cricket grounds. It was only there, when he wasn't playing or practising, that I was allowed to swing my father's oiled bat. At home it sat in a pail of bat oil and was strictly off limits to his children. This bat was the real deal. I cherished those moments at the cricket grounds when I could hit the hardball and score runs on the sidelines with other youngsters. My dad was not the only cricket player in the family. His father, Johnny, was from Westmoreland Parish, the most western part of the island, and was recruited by Monymusk to work on the sugar cane farm and play for the cricket team. Papa Johnny's father, who we never met, came from India. Most people don't know that Subban is an Indian name.

When the Team West Indies cricket games were broadcast on the transistor radio, everything stopped. Even better was watching those cricket games on the television at the community centre—when the TV was working. Those were the only times I watched TV. Cricket was in my blood, and it became the thing that I loved to do at school and away from school. We played wherever we could. We played in the yard at my mom's parents' house when my grandparents were away at the Alley market on Friday and Saturday. It drove my grandmother crazy because we'd damage the flowers that lined the walkway to her house. There were tidal salt plains in the area, and when the tide was out, the kids would go there and create teams. Even though it was a toxic dust bowl at times, it was flat and made for a good cricket pitch.

I could not use my dad's bat during our street games, so I learned how to make my own. At first I used scrap pieces of wood, but eventually I went into the bush and found a lignum vitae tree, the national tree of Jamaica. The wood is among the toughest in the world. Back then, I just called it a cricket bat tree. I'd use a machete to cut a limb that was the right thickness and length. Then I would use the machete and other tools to cut, shape, shave and polish it into my most prized possession. For our ball, my friends and I would cut bicycle tubes into elastic band shapes and stretch them over crumpled pieces of newspaper. We would place more and more elastic band tubes over the ball until it became harder and harder. Soon, it would take the shape we wanted and, like artists, we worked it to make it just right. Wickets were made of sticks, or we used whatever was convenient, such as a piece of furniture or a large rock.

I spent many hours playing pickup cricket with my friends. My eldest brother, Hopeton, tells me Mom always knew where to find me in our district. She just had to listen for the cheering, yelling and the crack of bat meeting ball. When I returned to Portland Cottage as an adult, many people remembered me as the kid who was always walking around with a cricket bat in his hand. I started the sport young and became good enough to be named captain of my school's junior team. I know that made my parents proud. My dad loved the sport, and he shared it with me. This shared love became another bond between us.

The West Indies cricket team, made up of the best players from the various islands, became role models for me. They inspired me to dream of one day playing for the West Indies and being the next Sir Garfield Sobers, one of the greatest cricketers of all time and captain of Team West Indies. Sobers was from Barbados, and he played in the 1950s, '60s and '70s. That was the first time I had a dream about being something, or somebody. I saw myself as a teenager going to Vere Technical High School, a big sports school in our district. But I'll never know how that would have played out, because life had other plans for me and my family.

The idea of moving to Canada was a seed that had been planted in my dad for quite a while. His brothers had moved to England to work in the mines, but the economy worsened there in the

1960s. However, there were jobs in North America for skilled tradesmen. My parents had high hopes for their children and for themselves—they wanted us to have more; they wanted us to *be* more. It was their drive to achieve, coupled with hope and ambition, that brought my family to Canada.

In 1970, my parents left Jamaica for Sudbury a few months before my brothers and me. At the send-off party, a goat was killed and some of it made into a soup called mannish water. There was rum punch and curried goat, served with rice and roti. It was quite a party. My parents had no worries about leaving us behind with my mom's parents, Vashtie and Edward Peters, who were like another set of parents to us. I remember the hot days when we were sitting in the shade and our grand-mother would call us to comb her hair. The breeze and the shade from the ackee tree, along with the comfort of having her hair combed, would soon send her to dreamland. We would comb her hair knowing she would fall asleep like a baby having a bottle. Before long we'd be on our own, doing something that burned more calories than combing grandma's hair.

Vashtie and Edward Peters

I have such vivid and happy memories of my time in Jamaica, but after we moved, I hardly returned over the next thirty years, only for a few funerals when I was in my teens. The next time I went back was with my mom when I was in my forties, and I'm so happy I made that trip because she died not long afterwards. Despite the decades that passed, going back was easy. Your childhood home never leaves you.

A lot has changed since I lived there, but a lot has stayed the same. Portland Cottage was, and is, a small place. Everyone knows everyone and each other's business. Today, you see more cars than bicycles. You don't see as many horse- or donkey-drawn carts. Everyone has a cellphone, of course—I didn't even *use* a telephone until I came to Canada. Everyone has more access to information than we did, but the closeness of the community has remained the same.

I don't think that core value of respecting your elders, however, has remained. But I see that in Canada too. I also don't see as many older people in the community. There isn't as much farming or fishing, either. I don't think people are helping themselves the way they did when I was growing up. People didn't have a lot, but they made the most of their situation—growing their food, for instance. Part of the problem has been a terrible drought. Many of the fruit trees are dying. There is still a lot of bartering and sharing, and it's still peaceful and safe to walk the streets. And the children still wear their school uniforms, like the one my mom made me for the trip to Dunn's River Falls.

Growing up we didn't have much, and sometimes I look back and think, *how did we survive that?* I've come to realize it is not where you live but how you live. We lived in a positive way with lots of love. Our house may have been small, but it was a home. It's not what you have but how you enjoy what you have; it's being thankful for what you have. Even though our family left for better opportunities, Jamaica was good to us. It was the best kind of foundation: built on the solid ground of working hard, setting goals and learning about perseverance.

3

The Making of a Canadian—
and a Canadiens Fan

A few years ago, when my dad, Sylvester, was seventy-five and living in Brampton, Ontario—forty-five years after he and my mom, Fay, had moved us from the southern coast of Jamaica to Northern Ontario—I asked him about our life in Sudbury. He said something I found very touching: "We had a good life in Sudbury," he said in his Jamaican patois. "I worked, we had something to eat and I raised my family there."

We had a good life in Sudbury. I couldn't have said it better myself.

Dad came to Canada in 1966 to work on the new Mack Truck assembly line in Oakville, Ontario, and sent money home to us, but he did not like his undocumented worker status, so he returned to Jamaica and started the proper procedures to emigrate. Also in 1966, my dad's brother Leslie moved to Sudbury to work at the Inco nickel mine as an electrician. Uncle Leslie and his wife, Aunty Irma, sponsored our family, and my dad arrived as a landed immigrant on June 10, 1970. By June 23 he had a job as a diesel mechanic at Falconbridge mine. He was twenty-nine years old. It was easy to find a job in the mines at that time, especially with the skills he had. Dad would work there for thirty years.

Mom came in July and quickly found a job at Sudbury Steam Laundry working as a seamstress. By the time I arrived in Sudbury at age twelve, with my two younger brothers, Patrick (Rex), ten, and Markel, eight, Mom was already working. Hopeton, who was fourteen, stayed in Jamaica with my grandparents and joined us in 1975.

Our plane landed in Toronto in August 1970. It was a Saturday, but Dad was at work. He was paid overtime for a Saturday shift and he never wanted to give up overtime, so he wasn't able to travel the five hours south to Toronto with Mom. At the laundry, Mom had recently met a Mrs. Gray and said to her, "I have to get the kids and I don't know how I am going to do it because Syl has to work." Mrs. Gray soon came back to my mom and said her husband would drive her. So, Mr. Gray drove my mom all the way to the Toronto airport and drove us back to Sudbury. I asked Dad to verify this story. He told me it

Dad working as a diesel mechanic

was true—and that Mr. Gray had refused to take gas money. He told my parents, "I'm an immigrant too." He was a miner at Inco and people had helped him when he came to Canada from Ireland. He was just giving back something others had given to him. I will never forget that act of generosity and kindness that greeted me and softened my heart to Canada.

That trip was our first time on an airplane. The only planes we had seen before were flying overhead. I remember the spinning propellers and the noise they created. A flight attendant accompanied us, as we were children travelling alone. The three of us couldn't sit together because there were only two seats per row. I can't recall what was served to eat, but it was different from what we were used to.

My first impression of Canada was the cold embrace of the artificially cooled air inside the airport terminal. It was immediately apparent that the feel and smell of the air was different. I had never experienced air conditioning before. Then I remember seeing my mom. I was looking at her through some bars. Either she was in some sort of cage or we were, and there was a metal fence we had to pass through before we could join her. I was so happy to be with Mom again! Another memory of that first day is Mr. Gray buying us a hot dog. I can't remember if it was at the airport or on the drive north, but it led to a story my brothers and I still laugh about today. When Mr. Gray asked if we wanted a hot dog, Rex said, "We don't eat dogs in Jamaica." The term *hot dog* was new to us—we knew them as wieners, but I had never had one before. It should come as no surprise I loved eating mine.

We first lived in Sudbury with Uncle Leslie and Aunty Irma at their house on Leslie Street. Theirs was another act of kindness I will never forget. If they hadn't sponsored us, I don't think there would be a Team Subban to talk about today. About a month later, my parents rented a house on Peter Street, now called Mountain Street.

A big part of our story in Sudbury was how people helped us. "The people were good and the experiences were good," Dad said. One of the most generous people was Madame Lil Dasty, now Madame Gagnon. She lived one street over on Leslie Street with her husband and two children, and she was our Welcome Wagon, explaining the lay of the land to my parents. Madame Lil worked as a secretary for a doctor in the Woolworth Building, and her doctor became our family doctor. She explained to us how to dress for winter. The first time I ate spaghetti was at her house. Her food became our food, and our food became their food too. I also remember her giving us hand-me-downs.

Today, Madame Lil is in her eighties and still keeps in touch. She has even gotten to know our children, especially

Taz, Natasha and P.K., because they often spent summers in Sudbury with my parents. When P.K. was playing junior hockey with the Belleville Bulls, they had a thrilling playoff game against the hometown Sudbury Wolves. Belleville lost in the third overtime and Sudbury advanced to the OHL championship. There was a bogus penalty call against P.K.—a hometown call if there ever was one—but I'm a parent, so I'm entitled to my opinion, right? After the game, the team was in the locker room. The players were obviously upset and were taking their time. A trainer or other team official was outside the locker room and Madame Lil, who was in her seventies then, came to him and said, "Can you tell P.K. I'm here?" So he goes in and says, "P.K., there's an old white lady waiting for you." Right away, P.K. knew it was Madame Lil and rushed out to greet her. P.K.'s hockey career had renewed that connection.

Living in Sudbury did take some adjustment. First of all, initially we had to stay inside, which was difficult for us because in Jamaica we were always outside. As we had arrived in either

Karl and Patrick in Sudbury

early or mid-August, it was several weeks before we started school. Mom was working, so during the day we stayed inside and watched TV and I cooked for my brothers. We were told not to make any noise.

I was definitely homesick. I missed Jamaica, my friends and the old ways, and now I was stuck inside, looking out. What I saw were kids who did not look like me. This made a significant impression. Jamaica was quite diverse; there were a few Jamaican white people as well as Chinese and Indian Jamaicans. Jamaicans came in different shades. Now I looked out my window and saw a lot of white people. I also saw the kids riding their bikes, something I didn't have. Everything was so new, so different. It wasn't long, however, until we started school, and after that we were allowed to go out and play with the kids in the neighbourhood and make friends.

Another transition was the language. Even though we speak English in Jamaica, it's patois, an English-based creole. Based on my age when I arrived, I should have been put in grade six, but in those days, new immigrants were automatically held back a grade, so I started school in Canada in grade five. Being older than the other kids bothered me, and it didn't exactly help the process of fitting in.

My first teacher, Mr. Kangas, was wonderful, however. He asked me to stand before the class and tell the other students about Jamaica. I got to do that two or three times, and it made me feel special. He'd say, "Karl, speak what you know." I would talk about the schooling and playing cricket and the fruit on the trees and going to the ocean, all those things that were native to me, that were of interest to me, that were a part of me. The kids would ask me questions. My experiences were so fresh in my mind and the kids wanted to know. Those things made me feel comfortable in school. Mr. Kangas used my own experiences to build my confidence, and his approach let the other kids get to know me. What a wonderful lesson for a future teacher to learn.

Another moment that stands out was in grade six, when we were making papier mâché out of newspapers. I needed more newspaper so I went to the teacher and asked, "Miss, where is the *Gleaner*?" She looked at me. "Where is the *Gleaner*?" I repeated. She kept on looking at me, clearly puzzled. I couldn't understand why she didn't understand me. The name of the newspaper in Jamaica is the *Daily Gleaner*. The word *newspaper* was foreign to me.

Besides my aunt and uncle, the Grays and Madame Lil, the kids on Peter Street also eased my transition from Jamaica to Canada, especially that first winter. And it was quite an adjustment. To think, only months earlier we'd left the hot weather, fruit trees and warm ocean for the thick boreal forest and rugged landscape of the Canadian Shield, home to moose, wolves, mile-deep nickel mines—and snow. I didn't know what snow was. I'd never seen snow on the pages of my books or on the TV screen in the community centre. I had never made the connection that the snow that would pile up in giant drifts on Sudbury's streets was essentially the same frozen water used to make the flavoured snowball treats we'd buy in Jamaica. A gentleman used to come around pushing a two-wheeled cart. Inside was a large block of ice, which he would shave with a wood planer and shape into a ball. Then he'd sprinkle strawberry syrup on it. Little did I know my future in Canada would be shaped and defined by snow and ice, and my cricket bat would be replaced by a hockey stick.

At the end of Peter Street was a school and an outdoor rink. Winter started early in those days, and once the cold weather came, the boards were put up and the skates taken out. I don't remember my first snowfall, but I probably experienced it walking to school. My dad remembers me walking home crying because I was cold, but we adapted and ended up loving the snow and winter because of the fun we would have. The kids on Peter Street immediately invited me to play road hockey and shinny on that large sheet of ice. I didn't have skates in those days, but I was encouraged to play in net wearing my winter boots. I was intrigued by the ice, by the notion that water could freeze outside. We also played a lot of competitive street hockey games on Peter Street, and in those, I didn't have to play net.

Sports offered a great way to integrate. I may not have been the best student in school, but being a good athlete helped me make friends and feel good about myself. I was able to fit in. I was Ken Dryden without skates. My parents eventually bought me skates from the Salvation Army, but by then I was a teenager and it was too late to catch up. I did learn to skate, but not well enough to play organized hockey. Here's the crucial thing about hockey: if you can't skate, you can't play. We also faced challenges getting equipment and paying fees. My parents were thirty years old with four kids to raise. Raising a hockey player was not in their pocketbook. They were working to catch up to their dreams for us and for themselves.

My love of hockey started by playing it with the neighbourhood kids, who were mostly francophone. Soon I was watching the local OHL team, the Sudbury Wolves, and listening to them on the radio. My best friend, Allan Peltoniemi, was a good player. We would go to the Sudbury Arena and watch the Wolves. I saw many future greats play, including Wayne Gretzky. I fell in love with the sport and desperately wished I could have been one of those OHL players. I never got the chance, but that love and desire to play was a force always simmering under the surface.

As for televised hockey, we had a limited choice of channels. There were two stations, the English station and the French station, and for whatever reason we got more broadcasts of the Montreal Canadiens than the Toronto Maple Leafs. Montreal was always playing on the French channel, and that's how I started watching. It led to arguments at home. My parents were new to Canada and here I was wanting to watch the games in French. They'd say, "You don't even understand what they are saying." Evenings were family time, and no one else wanted to watch a hockey broadcast in a language they didn't understand.

That's how my love for the Canadiens grew. It didn't hurt that Montreal had great teams in the 1970s. In the spring of 1971, Ken Dryden was called up from the AHL just before the playoffs and was a surprise starter in the post-season. He had a legendary playoff run as a rookie, frustrating the defending champs, the high-scoring Boston Bruins, in the first round, and it was thrilling to watch the Stanley Cup final against the Chicago Black Hawks. That season ended when Montreal won Game 7 on the road, and Dryden was named the series MVP. Move over, cricket and Garfield Sobers, and make room for hockey and Ken Dryden.

During our games on Peter Street, if the kids didn't want me to understand something they'd say it in French. But I did pick up some words—including some colourful ones I probably should not have known—because I was with them all the time and they would invite me into their homes to eat. We also played lacrosse and all the other schoolyard games together.

One thing that did bother me at the time was hearing people say that black people couldn't play hockey because we had weak ankles that made it impossible to skate well. How did I deal with this at a time when my most important job was to fit in with the crowd? In public I laughed it off, but privately I wanted to prove them wrong. I made a decision not to be bitter but to prove to them that I was better than their personal judgment of me or the group of people they identified me with.

When I looked at my friends and then looked at myself, both inside and out, I saw no evidence to support their weak ankle theory. I knew it must be false. I never thought of it as racism. No one teased me, but the so-called theory stuck with me and conflicted with the person I was developing into: I believed in myself, my abilities and my potential. I don't associate any of my experiences in Sudbury with race. No one said I couldn't play hockey because I was black. All of my friends were white, and they invited me to play. It wasn't a blow to my self-esteem but a boost to my determination to prove them wrong.

Most importantly, I was proving to myself that I was right. I didn't stop playing hockey. I didn't stop watching hockey. I continued to see myself in the game the same way the boys on Peter Street saw themselves in the game—playing, having fun, competing and living the dream through my favourite player. My interest in hockey continued to grow with the birth of Team Subban. Maria and the girls and I skated as a family, and when the boys came we took the interest to another level. The weak ankle theory died and was buried a long time ago.

Being introduced to ice hockey was a defining moment that made a young immigrant from Jamaica feel like a Canadian. A second defining moment came when we actually became Canadian citizens. It was in 1974, four years after our arrival. I was sixteen, and I remember all of us travelling down to the Post Office dressed in suits. I cried when we sang "O Canada." It is a moment I will never forget. I was lucky enough to become a Canadian twice—the day I was introduced to ice hockey and the day I received my citizenship.

The environment in Sudbury was right in so many ways for growing young people. We had few distractions. Maybe it was because we were busy picking blueberries and crabapples, playing hockey, lacrosse, baseball or football. We were too preoccupied with fun to find trouble. The saying "an idle mind is a playmate for the devil" did not apply to us. We had no idle time.

During those years we also were given more freedom and responsibilities. Mom worked, so she no longer stayed home with us like she had in Jamaica. My parents would leave for their jobs early in the morning and return around suppertime. We were home when they left in the morning and when they returned. My parents would make supper, or I would make supper. It was an expectation and a responsibility that I embraced—after all, I loved cooking and loved eating.

As I got older and started middle school, a new dream began to emerge. I developed an interest in basketball. My dad's mom, Edna Williams, had moved to Toronto. We would visit her several times a year, and we took advantage of the trip to buy clothes and food in Kensington Market that we couldn't get in Sudbury, such as goat meat and tropical fruits and fish. My grandmother was in her seventies, but she had TV channels that we didn't. It was while visiting her that I saw my first NBA game on TV. I would sit there for hours on a Saturday or Sunday afternoon watching NBA games. I remember seeing the Los Angeles Lakers play; I was mesmerized by Kareem Abdul-Jabbar's skyhook. Even today I am known for my hook shot, and that is where it started. While these trips to Toronto were important shopping excursions for my parents, access to televised NBA games topped my list of needs.

Before my parents could afford to buy a car, the family would hitch a ride with a friend named Sunny. My parents would pay for the gas and Mom would provide sandwiches for the journey. There was no GPS at the time, so Sunny would follow the Greyhound bus from the depot in downtown Sudbury all the way to Toronto. We never got lost. When the bus stopped in Parry Sound (the home of Bobby Orr!) we would stop too, to stretch, use the washroom and get gas.

In grade seven, I attended Lansdowne Public School and I tried out for the basketball team. I was cut. I saw myself as a good athlete, so being cut hurt me. But rather than be discouraged, I decided it wasn't going to keep me down. I just had to work hard before the grade eight tryouts.

I went to the schoolyard courts and started putting in the practice every day—whether it was thirty degrees Celsius or three degrees, I was out on that court working on my game. The next year I made the team, and that's when my basketball career started to blossom.

Later, I brought my basketball training to my house. My parents had a wooden pole for stringing a clothesline. I dug a hole in the yard and stuck the pole in the hole. Then I bought a rim and attached it to the pole. I spent hours in the back-yard playing basketball, working on my jump hooks, shoot-ing foul shots, honing my moves. I skipped rope. I can't count the thousands of skips I did per day. Before my parents fin-ished the basement, I'd go downstairs and work on my drib-bling skills. I'd listen to CKSO radio, and I came up with a routine where I'd perform a different drill for each song that came on. If a song was two minutes long, I'd be doing figure eights for two minutes. In the evening, when Mom was get-ting ready for bed because she had to get up early to work, she would be pounding on the floor, yelling, "Karl! Stop bounc-ing the ball!"

I saw a promotional ad for a basketball training program in a magazine, so I sent away for it, then religiously followed every step. Those drills were so ingrained I later used some of them to train Taz and Tasha in basketball and my sons in hockey. The drills involved jumping and running, such as jumping on the spot and lifting my knees to my chest. One running drill involved setting up pylons on a field. I'd sprint thirty yards, then jog ten, sprint sixty, jog ten and finally sprint ninety yards. I started out doing three sets and added a set a week until I was running seven sets, three times a week. I added a weighted vest to make it even tougher. Besides the training program I mailed away for, I also signed out books from the library on how to shoot by basketball legends John Havlicek and Pete Maravich. I was my own first coach.

Basketball had another influence on me. I struggled in

school when I first moved to Canada. Most kids who struggle do so for one of two reasons: either they are not motivated, or they feel they don't have the skills. In my case, I wanted to learn, but I still struggled with reading. My love for basketball led me to want to read about basketball, so Mom paid for a subscription to a monthly magazine called *Basketball Digest*. As I started to dream about becoming an NBA player, sometime around middle school, I wanted to read about NBA players. I figured if I knew more about them, practised liked them, trained like them, maybe I could become them. I realize today how much *Basketball Digest* helped my reading, along with my ability to play the game.

One of the players I idolized was Marvin Barnes, a star with Providence College who was selected second overall by Philadelphia in the 1974 NBA draft after leading the nation in rebounding during his senior year. I liked the way he played and I especially liked that he had a lot of personality. Barnes initially played for two years in the American Basketball Association for St. Louis and later with four NBA teams.

During Malcolm's first year playing goalie for the Providence Bruins in the 2013–14 season, Maria and I went to see him play at their home arena, the Dunkin' Donuts Center. Hanging from the rafters were banners, and my eyes stopped at No. 24, Marvin Barnes. The arena is also home to the Friars, the Providence College basketball team. Barnes's number was retired in 2008. Sadly, Marvin was a great talent who had lifelong drug and alcohol addictions. He died in September 2014 at age sixty-two. His story shows that you can make it in basketball but you also have to make it in life. Of course, I didn't know about his troubles when I was a teenager, but it is important to have people you look up to and aspire to be. You are reaching to achieve at their level, and there is nothing wrong with that.

When I was in high school, my parents bought a new build in a subdivision outside Sudbury in the town of Val Caron. My parents lived at 3858 Velma Street for thirty years. They loved the house, and their many friends would come over all the time. They had white friends and black friends. There were mining friends and friends from Mom's new workplace, Sudbury Memorial Hospital. She had gone back to school and gotten a job as a lab technician at the hospital. Mom and Dad enjoyed entertaining, and there was always lots of food, drinks and music.

Our house was always a fun place, but it was far away from my Sudbury high school, which I wanted to keep attending. I played volleyball for the school because I liked the sport, but I also read it would make me a better basketball player due to the jumping and timing required. I became a good player because I worked hard, and so the volleyball coach, Terry Kett, arranged for another teacher who lived nearby to give me a ride to school that year. To get home, I needed to take the late bus, which wasn't a City of Sudbury bus, and it was costly and ran at irregular times. The next year I had to take the bus to and from school. To pay for bus fare I needed to get a job. That is how I ended up working at the A&P grocery store. My parents, like all good parents, were concerned that having a job after school created too long a day for me. I was determined to make it work, so I made it work. I did what I had to do, and my parents respected me for it, despite their concerns. I was learning you could achieve things if you set your mind to it.

I started working at the A&P as soon as I turned sixteen. I hated bothering my parents all the time for money, and I knew I could fit the job into my schedule. I was paid $2.75 an hour and worked about fifteen to twenty hours a week. Having that job taught me some valuable lessons as a young man. One was the importance of working for what you want.

I learned another lesson that has stayed with me to this day. I worked alongside another part-timer cleaning the store on Tuesday evenings. He told me one night the manager had asked him to keep an eye on me. I said, "What do you mean, 'Keep an eye on me'? I'm not doing anything. I come to work, I work hard and I go home." Soon after, perhaps the next week, he repeated his warning at the start of our shift. A few hours later I was cleaning the lunchroom when the manager and the area manager called us both to the front office and said one of us was breaking the seal on the soft drink bottles and looking for the winning cap in the "dream home" competition. I said it wasn't me. I could see why I was under suspicion. Everyone liked my colleague, who was in charge of the shift, and there were only the two of us working.

Soon after that meeting the other guy confessed. I almost fainted. I couldn't believe it. He was the last guy I thought would do something like that. This event opened my eyes. I learned a very valuable lesson about trust that I passed on to my kids: You have to trust people in life, but you also have to be wary. People are capable of doing almost anything, and nothing should shock or surprise you. I still trust people, but at the same time, I don't trust anybody, if that makes sense. Even my own kids. If they ever did something bad, I wouldn't be shocked. You should never be surprised at what people are capable of doing. Luckily, that works both ways; people can surprise you in a positive fashion too.

A final lesson I learned while working at the A&P was that I did not want to work at the A&P the rest of my life. There were lots of things I liked about the job: bagging groceries, the conversations, putting groceries in people's trunks and helping customers find items on the shelves. I knew at that age that I liked serving the public, working for people. But I also knew I wanted to do more and to be more.

To better ourselves, to have the opportunity to do more with our lives, is why my parents moved to Sudbury. They also helped their family. My Uncle Leslie's act of generosity in sponsoring my parents led to my parents sponsoring others to come to Canada, including my grandmother, Vashtie. She moved to Sudbury in 2000 after my mom died of breast cancer at age fifty-nine. My grandmother was a widow and came for her daughter's funeral, a day that was so hard on her. My dad sponsored her and she was able to stay in Canada. After she died in 2006, we flew her body back to Jamaica to be buried beside her husband.

I asked my dad about the challenges he and my mom faced coming to Canada. He told me he was concerned about my mom having to work outside the home. He was not sure how she would adapt. But Mom was from a blue-collar family and she knew what hard work was. She grew up seeing it from her parents and grandparents.

I also asked him what he thinks he and Mom passed on to their children. He said: working hard, being respectful and being intelligent. If the school ever had to call home because we weren't doing our homework, that was not good. But if they called because we weren't being respectful, to my parents that was worse. They did not want us to let them down, and we didn't either; we made them feel proud of us.

I saw this when I had success in sports. There were articles in the newspaper or my name would be on the radio for being a high scorer in a high-school game. My parents would hear it and feel good because we were succeeding at something. Our family was living the Canadian dream my parents had visualized in a small town in Jamaica. My dream, however, my life's passion, had not been born yet. It was still inside of me, waiting to be awakened, like a sleeping giant. That was about to change.

Patrick, Karl, Markel, Sylvester and Fay

4

Waking the Sleeping Giant

I moved to Thunder Bay, Ontario, in 1979 harbouring a big dream—to play basketball in the NBA. As we drove from Sudbury, ten hours through the almost endless forests of north-western Ontario to Lakehead University, I had no way of knowing that another dream was waiting for me.

Thunder Bay is a remote industrial city of 110,000 hardy souls, built on the rocky shores of Lake Superior, the world's largest freshwater lake. There used to be two cities—Port Arthur in the north and Fort William in the south—but they merged in 1970 to become Thunder Bay. Across the bay from the city is a peninsula with a massive land formation called the Sleeping Giant because it looks like a man lying on his back with his arms folded across his chest. The giant's cliffs rise as high as 240 metres above the dark, cold lake.

I was recruited to play basketball for the Lakehead University Nor'Westers by Don Punch, who coached me at Sudbury Secondary. Don, who was also a teacher of mine, took a job at Lakehead before my grade thirteen year and wanted me to join him in Thunder Bay after I graduated. Lakehead wasn't the only university interested in me coming out of high school. George Burger, the athletic director at the University of Prince Edward Island, wanted me to move out east, and Mansfield State, a northern Ohio school that is part of the University System of Ohio, had also offered me a scholarship. I decided Lakehead was for me. I liked Don, and my high-school friend Ned Janjic went to Lakehead to play as well.

My dream of becoming an NBA player was powerful. I woke up every day living that dream, or thinking about it, working to fulfill it. It was so far deep into my soul that I left no stone unturned in trying to realize that dream. Still, because I was rarely able to watch games on TV growing up, I didn't benefit from the exposure of watching college and professional players in action. Arriving at Lakehead, I wasn't coming from a position of strength in terms of fulfilling my dream. What I did know was I needed to play in university if I wanted to make it to the NBA.

The idea wasn't completely far-fetched. A star Lakehead player who graduated a year before I arrived, Jim Zoet, did manage to get a taste of that dream. The seven-foot-one centre played in Thunder Bay for two seasons, 1976–77 and 1977–78, joining the team after playing three seasons at Kent State University on a scholarship. Zoet averaged nineteen points a game, was named an all-Canadian player in both of his seasons with the Nor'Westers and led Lakehead to its first Canadian Interuniversity Athletic Union championship game in his first season. After graduating from Lakehead, Zoet played for the 1980 Canadian Olympic men's basketball team.

While he remained undrafted by the NBA, Zoet did have the thrill of putting on a Detroit Pistons jersey in 1982 (No. 40), playing in seven games that season on a team with stars such as Isiah Thomas, Bill Laimbeer, Vinnie Johnson and Kelly Tripuka. He also played professionally in Europe, Latin America and the Philippines.

I began saving for university when I started grade thirteen. I gave my mom my paycheques from working at the A&P to put away for school. When it was time to leave for Thunder Bay, my mom handed me $700. Ned and I drove to Thunder Bay with my childhood friend Micho Srdanovic, who was also attending Lakehead. Micho was around fifteen when his dad died in a mining accident. He inherited his father's grey Pontiac Laurentian, a car that years later would take us away to school.

I travelled light in those days, packing one gym bag with my basketball gear and two garbage bags containing my clothes. We arrived in Thunder Bay on a Thursday in mid-August, and by Monday morning all that money was gone— and it wasn't spent on rent, books and tuition. I had a great time with my old friends and a few new teammates that weekend. Even though I wasn't the only one bankrolling the good times, I learned I could not spend my time or money that way, as it left me playing catch-up all year. I didn't tell my parents about my shopping spree on fun and would not have dared to ask them for money.

Once school started, however, it was time to get to work. I knew I had to be good in school if I wanted to be good at basketball, that the discipline required to excel in the classroom would also be needed on the hardwood. Being good was as easy as saying ABC. *A* is for regular attendance in school. *B* is for good behaviour. *C* is for completing schoolwork. I think I was one of the few guys on the team who passed his courses that first year.

I wasn't a natural basketball player, but what I knew was that I had to work very hard at it. Before practice and after practice, I would be in the gym skipping or lifting weights. In the summer I stayed in Thunder Bay, and I would spend my free time running sprints in the field beside the gym.

I had a pretty good first year playing for the Nor'Westers, and in the summer of 1980, before the start of my second year, one of the things I did to support myself was work at the Lakehead University Abitibi-Price basketball camp. That's where I discovered I was a natural at working with kids, and the kids loved working with me because they found I was approachable and friendly. What they probably didn't know was that I liked them more. I got a lot out of it. In my first year, I had studied business and took some physical education courses, but I hadn't known where I wanted to go academically. After working at the basketball camp that summer, I realized I loved working with children, so in my second year I started taking courses that would lead me to a teaching degree.

As I started down this path, I was also beginning to realize that the basketball dream wasn't going to become a reality. In life we make plans and the plans don't always work out. It's not because of a lack of effort, that's just the way it is. Dreams are necessary, but you have to recognize the signs when they are not ultimately achievable.

I was a pretty good player. I was a Great Plains Athletic Conference first- or second-team all-star in four of my five years at Lakehead. I led the league in rebounding one year. I led my team in scoring one year and was team MVP twice. But for all that success, I never made the junior national team, and that meant the NBA was not going to be a possibility. Of course I felt some disappointment, but because I'd found something else I knew I wanted to do, I was okay letting the basketball dream go.

This experience I was having brings me to an important point: what is inside of us determines what is ahead of us. Thunder Bay illustrated this perfectly for me, thanks to the Sleeping Giant, which I could see from my apartment in downtown Port Arthur. We all have a sleeping giant inside of us—it's another way to think of our potential. We must find the thing that awakens it and brings it to life. It was in Thunder Bay, at Lakehead University, that I discovered my giant and brought it to life: working with children and being an educator would become my passion.

During my first year at Lakehead, my high-school teammate Ned and I lived at 87 Matthew Street. The house had three bedrooms, although in my case that was a misnomer since I didn't even own a bed. I slept with a comforter on the floor. Ned had the second room and teammate Wayne Como and his girlfriend Enis shared the third. There were months we ran out of money and couldn't afford to pay for the oil truck to come and fill up the tank to heat the place. You want to know what cold is? We sure did, living in Thunder Bay in the fall and winter without oil for the furnace. But we had good times that year, and the visiting teams would come to our house and party.

I needed to work while attending school, and I was able to get a transfer from the A&P store in Sudbury to the one on River Street in Thunder Bay, which today is part of the Metro grocery chain. I was now making good money, about eleven dollars an hour, which was decent pay in the early 1980s.

But working at the A&P was always going to be a means to an end. This became crystal clear to me one day in the meat room. I used to have to clean the meat-cutting machines, which didn't have a nice smell by the end of the day. I was cleaning the chicken out of the machine and I remember saying to myself, *I am not going to be doing this for the rest of my life. I'm only doing it now to put myself through school. I know what I'm going to be doing.* Sometimes we have to do jobs or tasks we don't like, but knowing why we are doing them helps to make it okay. And I knew why I was doing it. I knew there was a lot more out there for me. Maybe I didn't know exactly what it was, but I knew I wanted more.

My A&P money enabled me to get my own apartment on Cumberland Street in downtown Port Arthur in my second year. I didn't want to live with anyone anymore: I was around my teammates all day and wanted some solitude at night. I think I paid $175 a month for a little bachelor apartment. I had my own room and bathroom, but I shared a kitchen and a shower

with two other apartments. Whenever I return to Thunder Bay
to play in Lakehead's alumni basketball game, I drive down
Cumberland Street and look at the old apartment building. It
hasn't changed.

It is so nice to go back to the city, relive the good times and
hang out with some old teammates. But the experience is also
bittersweet. The alumni game is named after a star player for
Lakehead, John Zanatta. I was very close with my teammates,
and Johnny was particularly important to me. I looked up to
Johnny, and not just because he was a model teammate—and
later my coach—but because he was also a model person. He
was married, he was a father and he was the type of person you
would want to marry your daughter. After he graduated, he
coached the team for three years. He wasn't much older than
we were, but we respected him.

At the time of our graduation, Johnny was the school's all-
time leading scorer (1,895 points in his career from 1976 to
1981). I had the assist on his basket that set the record. I will
never forget that moment. We also had fun together off the court.
Johnny took me fishing. He was from Sault Ste. Marie and loved
to fish. We both stayed in Thunder Bay in the summer, and he
would come pick me up around 3 a.m. and we'd drive to these
fishing spots he knew. We'd catch pike and walleye. I would soak
the pike in salt water and cook it. The guys would love it.

After leaving Lakehead, Johnny moved to London, Ontario,
to teach. The last time I saw him was at Pearson Airport in
Toronto after we had both played in an alumni basketball game.
The following summer, in 1990, we received devastating news:
Johnny had been driving back to Thunder Bay to teach and
coach at the summer basketball camp there when he was killed

in a car accident. He was only thirty-three years old. I received many awards from my playing days at Lakehead—trophies and watches—but the best gift came from Johnny who, in my final year, gave me a photo of me in action on the basketball court. Of all the things I was given, I value that the most because it came from him.

Johnny was a big inspiration to me. He graduated a teacher and so did I. He was a great father to his children and a good husband. He set a standard I've always aspired to, and he touched the lives of so many in the short time he had. Wherever he is, I know he is looking at us. I hope he's saying, "I did a good job with the guys I was in charge of."

My teammates were so important to me during those years. I had a closeness with them that I didn't have with my classmates because we lived together, we sacrificed together, we ate together, we were hungry together—our friendship was bigger than basketball. My teammate Tony Scott was the best man at my wedding, and he's godfather to my oldest daughter. We were like brothers. If I didn't have enough to eat, he would share what he had. If he didn't have enough, he knew he could come to my place. That's the way we lived.

I seem to have a lot of memories of not having enough to eat. I was the cook among my group of friends. I would buy a couple cans of sardines and make some macaroni and cheese with Jamaican dumplings. My teammates loved it, probably because they were so hungry. When we travelled, the team would give us five or ten dollars a day for food. We'd travel in a van eight hours to Winnipeg and sometimes they wouldn't give us money but just hand out sandwiches instead. We'd complain loud and long. Did I mention we were always hungry?

None of us were on scholarships, so we had to work hard for everything we had. Nothing was given to us but an opportunity to play basketball, which we all loved to do.

Even though we were obsessed with basketball, some of that friendship and competitiveness spilled over onto the hockey rink. I may have been playing basketball, studying to become a teacher and working at the A&P, but my love for hockey was always there. I got the chance to play intramural ice hockey. A lot of the players on the basketball team were from Northern Ontario and Winnipeg and were good skaters. Johnny Zanatta had tried out for the London Knights of the OHL.

The Lakehead house league was the most competitive hockey I have ever played, and I wasn't as good a skater then as I am today, now that I've put in so many hours on the ice with my children. I have to admit, I didn't enjoy playing the house league games; the skating was difficult and when I fell, it hurt—a lot. I played with borrowed equipment that was either too big or too small. I played defence, but I didn't move much—I was more like a totem pole. This was one of the times I didn't have bragging rights. On the basketball court we'd all be big talkers; on the ice I was silent. Little could I imagine that my skating would one day improve so much that I would end up coaching my children in the Greater Toronto Hockey League for ten years.

I graduated after four years at Lakehead and then continued on to study at its teacher's college for a year to earn my bachelor of education. My new dream of becoming a teacher and working with children was starting to become a reality.

Student teachers don't know a lot until they stand up in front of a bunch of real, live students. Those first teaching experiences are called your practicals. My first time in the classroom in Thunder Bay was tough and humbling. I was placed in a school for three or four weeks. At first, we observed the teacher. Then he or she would have us teach an easy lesson. After that, we had to take on a more difficult lesson.

The first teacher I was assigned to, and I wish I could remember his name, was hard on me. My first class was a primary class, I think grade three. The school had an open concept design, like my first school in Jamaica. The walls had been removed and the classrooms were separated by furniture. The students sat at round tables set up around the room. The teacher's desk was placed among the students' desks, not at the front of the class. My supervisor would sit at his desk and observe me teaching the students at a designated meeting place on the carpet. I don't know if the students knew how nervous I was, but I know they had me pegged as a rookie the minute they laid eyes on me.

I couldn't seem to do anything right, and I was not enjoying the experience. I think my supervisor wanted to send a message: "This is serious business; you have to get it right." He really drove me, and thanks to his dedication to the profession, he helped me mature. At first I kicked back, but he kept pushing. He was very thorough—my lesson plans would have red marks all over them. He was stressing the point that a lesson plan has to be good on paper before you put it into action. We'd prepared lesson plans at teacher's college, but it was totally different in the real world.

This was a time for learning and growing and getting feedback, which wasn't always easy to hear. Whether you are an athlete or student, and I was both at that time, feedback can be hard to take, especially when you see it as something that makes you look and feel bad. I didn't realize it then, but feedback is the breakfast of champions. I learned that becoming a champion teacher does not happen overnight—it takes time. And this teacher didn't care that I was Karl Subban, star basketball player at Lakehead University. He knew I needed to become Mr. Subban, who would have to command the attention and respect of a classroom of students.

We had a number of practicals, and the instructors and schools would change, but after that first experience it became easier for me because of the standard set by that first teacher. The bar was set very high, and as they say, the bar you set is the bar you achieve. I know deep down I wanted to be the best teacher I could be, but I didn't know what that entailed. I learned early that teaching was going to be difficult and require hard work, but that was one thing I was never afraid of.

Your university years are tough. They test you not only as a scholar but as a person. To succeed you need to seek out inspiration from the lives of those you look up to. One of those people during my time in Thunder Bay was someone I never had the chance to meet: Terry Fox. Terry and I were born in the same year, 1958. Terry was at Simon Fraser University when I was at Lakehead, and he had been a basketball player too. I thought we had a lot in common. In 1980, I followed his cross-country Marathon of Hope, a journey he undertook to raise money to fight cancer. And when his run ended just outside Thunder Bay, it was very emotional for me. All Canadians were awed by his courage. We wanted to be part of his mission, and people across the country lined the highways to see him, to show him that he wasn't alone.

I'll never forget the first time I visited the Terry Fox monument just outside Thunder Bay. It has since been moved to higher ground above the highway and is adjacent to a rest stop and more parking, but when I first saw his statue it stood right beside the Trans-Canada Highway, overlooking the dense forest that spreads out down to the shores of Lake Superior. I could feel the power of the man there.

Terry provided many memorable quotes, but there is one that stands out for me, something he said after being asked how he managed to run a marathon every day: "I just kept running to the next telephone pole and when I got there I would focus on the next pole." He dreamed big but he took small steps—which he had to do because of his artificial right leg—one pole to the next. It's an approach we can all learn from when we set out to accomplish our dreams. Terry Fox's Marathon of Hope may have ended in Thunder Bay, but his dream did not die there. Through his foundation it has lived on and grown larger, passing on to new generations who keep his name and cause alive.

It so happened that Thunder Bay was where my own dream was born, where I discovered my passion. One of the most important lessons I learned was that what I first planned—my first dream—was not what I was meant to do. My association with hockey is important, and it is how I am known to most people, but it's my career as an educator that defines who I am as a person and makes me who I am. Sometimes in life, the plans we make don't work out, but if you stay true to the spirit behind them, they can lead to something better.

5

A Difference Maker

All through my childhood, adolescence and university years, sports consumed my time, focus and energy. But once I became a fully responsible, working adult, my favourite sport was no longer on a pitch, field, court or ice rink. My new arena was the classroom.

Teaching drove me to be the very best I could be. I was not satisfied, however, with being a teacher as stated on my certificate. Our children needed more. Our schools needed more. Our society needed more. Very early in my teaching career, I came to the conclusion that I needed to be more of a difference maker.

With that in mind, I set out not to be just the best teacher I could be, but also to have the greatest impact I could on the lives around me.

I've worked with children from a young age. It started with babysitting and transitioned into coaching. At Sudbury Secondary School, in my senior year, I was assistant coach to the midget boys' volleyball team. My vice-principal was the head coach, but because of his busy work schedule I took over most of the duties. While I was at Lakehead University, I coached children at basketball clinics, and also high-school and fellow university students in summer leagues.

My relationship with children is like the relationship between magnet and steel. Children have always seemed to like me, and I would like them a little bit more. That strategy seemed to work for me in growing positive relationships over my career.

One time, a young student made me look deep inside myself. I'd just made a presentation to a student body during Black History Month and a question and answer session followed. A girl came up, about eight, barely reaching the microphone as she asked, "Mr. Subban, why do you love children so much?"

This girl did not know it, but she'd thrown me a curveball of a question. I don't remember how I replied, but I knew it wasn't what I wanted to say, or what I truly meant. Swing and a miss.

This was a wet paper bag I needed to fight my way out of. The little girl's question was riding my mind like a jockey for about three weeks. It wasn't until I took a deep dive into who I was and what I believed that I came up with the answer I was looking for. If that young student is reading my book, I want to tell her that the reason I love children as much as I do is because love is the most important thing I can give to her, or any child.

When you love children, they will love you back. If you want children to care about what you say or do, you must communicate and demonstrate that you care about them. That caring stays with them and stays in them like the oxygen we breathe. Whenever a child told me, "I love you, Mr. Subban" or "I like you, Mr. Subban," I would instantly reply, "I love you more" or "I like you more."

So, with this love for children, pursuing a career in teaching seemed like a logical move. I made a decision early on, however, that despite my love for sports, it would have been too easy for me to teach physical education. I wanted to teach reading and writing and math and science. In fact, I loved science so much, I later earned a number of certificates in science from York University. I didn't want to be perceived as the jock in the classroom. I wanted to be Karl Subban, the teacher in the classroom.

Cordella Junior Public School in Toronto was my first home as a teacher. Comprising kindergarten to grade six, it's where I worked my first six years, from 1985 to 1991. The first children I taught were in a split class, grades four and five, and during that first year of teaching, leading those young students felt like driving on a city street with many stop signs. I would start a lesson or activity, but then I would have to stop because I could see the children were not engaged—so I needed to start all over again. Go. Stop. Go. Stop. Stopping and starting is a good thing. Just as you don't want to drive through a stop sign, it's not advisable to carry on with a lesson or activity that is not working. I learned early on in my teaching career to obey the signs, especially the red ones.

After about four years of teaching, a good friend of mine, a colleague in the classroom next door, had been assigned to teach a split grade three and four class, a group whose bad reputation preceded them. The prospect stressed the teacher out so much that she'd refused the assignment and threatened to leave the school. I valued our friendship on a personal level and wanted to support her professionally too.

So, without a lot of soul searching, I volunteered to teach this group of twenty-one students who had a reputation for being needy academically, socially and emotionally. I called them the Class of 21. Out of these twenty-one students, nineteen came from a single-parent home. I could have come up with twenty-one reasons why I should not have taken on a teaching assignment that ought to have been reserved for a veteran staff member. But I held a strong belief I could make a difference to these students as their teacher, so I jumped at the opportunity.

The unfortunate thing about teaching, sometimes, is that a class can get a reputation for being terrible, and then that reputation can become a self-fulfilling prophecy. For whatever reason, some teachers are better than others at working with children who have big challenges. Some teachers prefer it when the kids come ready to learn and ready to co-operate, but in my experience, the majority of kids need the teacher to make extra efforts to get them involved in the learning process.

I felt I was up for the challenge. I believed these students did not see themselves as being good at school. This is the most damaging of all the labels students can give themselves. Children need to know what they are good at. This was a conflict that was swallowing them. I am not sure what others saw in them, but I know what I saw: I saw their potential to become better. I believed in them and believed they were capable of producing more. I wanted to become their loving, caring teacher who believed they could do better.

I was a young teacher in the profession, but I was a veteran when it came to hard work, dedication and determination. I remember being told that the first five years of teaching are about learning how to teach. I did not have five years. The children in my care were needy and greedy for someone to make a positive difference in their lives today, not tomorrow. There were many days when I left work feeling stressed, tired and rushed, but also more determined than ever. I took ownership of those boys and girls. They were *my* kids, and they were in obvious need of a difference maker in their lives.

To get to know them better and to strengthen our relationship, I would bring Karl Subban the person—separate from Mr. Subban the teacher—into the classroom. I loved making kites, so we made kites together. I enjoyed cooking and baking, so we cooked and baked. At the end of each month we'd bake a cake, from scratch, usually a carrot cake with cream cheese icing, to celebrate all the birthdays that month. My mom gave me the recipe and instructions. And it was through these students that I discovered my own recipe for personal and professional success as an educator, parent and coach, a way to touch hearts, stimulate minds and engage hands.

Taking charge of the atmosphere in the classroom is one thing, but the outside world is another matter. I learned that year that kids are capable of doing a lot more than we give them credit for. In the middle of that school year, the children were about to complete a social studies unit on Australia, and the final activity was to go see an Australian-themed play at Toronto's Young People's Theatre. Some of my colleagues tried to persuade me not to take the Class of 21 on this field trip. The common refrain was that these children did not deserve to go because of their not-so-positive track record, and they were bound to turn this positive educational experience into a disaster: they were going to act up and be disruptive. They were going to embarrass the school.

I had a different opinion. First, I set the tone and the expectations with the class. I told them we were going to the theatre and I wanted them all to wear their nicest clothes and to be on their best behaviour. I also shared with them that some people didn't believe they could go on this trip and listen, co-operate and learn, which sparked their competitive spirit. The children in the class were now bent on proving everyone wrong.

The day of the field trip my class arrived at school looking special in their Sunday best. We were off to a good start. At the theatre, they were the best-dressed group of kids and they behaved well, living up to the expectations I had set for them. They were not like some other kids there, who were running around as if they were on an extended recess. Their behaviour matched the way they looked. I told the Class of 21 that they could behave well, and that's what they did, making the outing a positive learning experience. I believed in them and they believed in me.

Throughout my career, I always set the same high standards for school trips. Once the school bus was full, I'd get on and stand at the front, quieting the excited voices. I'd say, "I have a good name and a good reputation, so don't ruin it. If you go and misbehave, they'll be calling Mr. Subban and asking me what kind of school I'm running. Please don't ruin my reputation. You know how long it took me to earn this reputation I have today?" And the kids took the message to heart. As an educator, I wanted to implant my voice in the back of each child's head, just as my parents had done with me.

Progress was slow with the Class of 21, but I did see evidence of improvement. One technique I employed and which I refined over the years was to develop relationships with the children. In education we like to talk about rapport, about making every child feel valued.

At the same time, I worked hard at improving my teaching, and was always seeking out books on the subject. Cordella was not far from the board office at the corner of Eglinton Avenue West and Keele Street. Some days I would drive there during the lunch hour and take out journals to read. I was trying to learn as much as I could, such as techniques on how to teach writing and the best ways of working with children whose first language was not English.

I tried to make my lessons as concrete and practical as possible, instead of theoretical. I tried thematic teaching, such as the unit on Australia. We'd also brainstorm as a class and I'd ask the students what *they* wanted to learn, and that is what we'd study, because it wasn't so much the content that was important, it was the skills. I wanted them to read; I wanted them to write; I wanted them to be present. Interactive, student-centred learning was the goal.

But the most important aspect of teaching the Class of 21 was reaching them, building a relationship with them and making sure they knew I cared about them. And I got to teach subjects that were fun for me, such as science. Little experiments are a wonderful way to open up a child's imagination. Besides making teaching fun and showing them I cared about them, I also set high expectations. Then I would give them the feedback they needed, the recognition and the praise when they showed growth.

The only thing I wish I'd had with that class was more parent involvement, because when parents are willing and able to pay attention to their children's learning, they'll point out your mistakes and make you better at your job. I'm good with criticism, as long as it's the constructive kind. I was still a new teacher. I know I made mistakes. To a certain extent, that's just part of teaching.

Those children were very demanding of me, but they learned that year—and so did I. Their behaviour got better and they lived up to my expectations. I knew they had it in them to learn and, if anything, I wish I could have been a better teacher, because those kids were ready to learn.

As a rookie teacher, I felt it was important to visit the staff room on a regular basis. The staff room is more than a refuge from the classroom—it's a place to talk and socialize and catch up on school business, to get yourself known. It reminded me of a sports team's locker room. The veteran teachers are the kings and queens—as a newer staff member you don't sit in their chairs and you don't try to dominate the conversations. It's the rookie's job to fall in line.

It didn't take me too long, however, to figure out I didn't always like the atmosphere in this locker room. The same topics would be chewed over ad infinitum: the problems with leadership and the problems with parents, who were either too involved or not involved enough. Or the talk would turn to the kids and their difficult behaviour.

Negativity can conquer any environment. I always saw the glass as half full, not half empty. I was never one to sit around complaining—it wasn't productive and it didn't feel right to me. I didn't want to catch the cold that was being spread.

Eventually, I made a decision to visit the staff room less often. I realized the conversations there never changed. I don't know who said this, but they were right on: "If you can't change the people around you, change who you are around." That is exactly what I did. My trips to the staff room were now on the same basis as those to my family doctor—only when necessary.

I want to stress that I liked my colleagues as people. They did a lot for me; for example, they pushed me to become curriculum chairperson. But I maintain that the chatter and negativity I saw in many staff rooms isn't good for young teachers, and it's not good for the morale of staff overall.

It's also not good for the school. Sometimes we had to warn staff to watch what they said because the educational assistants or others in the building might overhear them. If you tell me a particular student never behaves and I get that child in my classroom, then that is where I am starting with the child. That is a danger. Instead of giving that child a chance—instead of giving yourself a chance to develop a relationship with that child, or, say, with a parent who you've heard is trouble—you've already been contaminated.

But there was one visit I did make to the staff room that was truly remarkable. Just before the beginning of recess one morning, I was summoned to meet with all the other teachers, who gathered in their usual places one by one. As soon as everyone was present, a senior staff member asked me to stand and then he made a speech: "Karl, we know that you have a very challenging group of children, a group that you volunteered to teach. We like the fact that you have never complained about your children's behaviour. You have remained so positive about them. And we'd all like to recognize you for that." The staff presented me with a "gold medal" made from cardboard with a piece of string attached so it could be worn around my neck. Written on my medal were the words: "CORDELLA'S #1 TEACHER."

I could not believe what was happening—a group of experienced teachers making the effort to recognize me for doing my job. It was a gesture that blew fresh wind into my sails, a golden moment that left me mostly speechless—but not emotionless. I know I thanked the staff for their medal of recognition with joy infusing every ounce of my being.

Praise raises you. It can sometimes be hard to find, whether at home or in the classroom. We all need that positive feedback to thrive, no matter how elusive it can be. It wasn't one big thing I did with the Class of 21; it was those small victories I looked for every day when working with my class. Sometimes I had to look through the eye of a needle to find something a student had done that was worthy of praise, but that is what the Class of 21 needed.

The medal I was presented by my colleagues may have been made of cardboard, but it was worth way more to me than its weight in gold.

———

I was focusing in my early years on being the best teacher I could be, and I guess my efforts were noticed. At the time, I wasn't thinking of going into administration, as it was still so early in my career. But that changed after a meeting I attended with a "difficult" parent and the local school board trustee, Steve Mould.

We met in the corner of the library. This father, who had three or four children in the school, including a daughter in my class, was wearing dark glasses. We couldn't see his eyes, but we could hear what he had to say. The details are foggy now, but it had something to do with race, and it was directed at the principal. I didn't think the man's criticism was fair, and I told him that what he was saying was just not so. Sometimes in education we feel handcuffed by all the policies and protocols, but perhaps I hadn't been in the profession long enough to let those bother me. By the end of the meeting, the matter was resolved, and all parties left feeling satisfied.

Afterwards, Trustee Mould said, "Karl, you know what? You should think about going into administration." He saw leadership in me—I hadn't been afraid to stand up and say what was right. Then, as now, I feel that when you are dealing with hot-button issues where two sides are far apart, you try to build a bridge so people, ideas and conversations can meet. You are not going to move ahead if you don't.

Not long after Trustee Mould encouraged me in the corner of the library to consider moving into administration, I enrolled in York University's principal's qualification course. I had only been teaching for three years. By year five, I was ready to apply for a vice-principal's position in the City of York Board of Education. I remember my final statement in the interview process. I took out a Polaroid picture of the teachers making their presentation to me. The interview team saw the cardboard award with the words printed in bold—CORDELLA'S #1 TEACHER—hanging around my neck. I told them that this recognition by my peers was one of the main reasons why I felt ready for a vice-principal's position. My application to become an administrator was successful. For the 1991–92 school year I became a vice principal-in-training at Roseland Junior School.

Through a lot of hard work and some good fortune, my professional life was taking off and I was living my dream of working with children in the classroom, helping to develop their hands and their minds. And as for my personal life, momentous things were most definitely in the works.

6

Parenthood

New Year's Eve is often filled with the excitement of the possibilities that lie ahead. We always hope the new year will be better than the one in the rear-view mirror. This was true on the night I bid farewell to 1984. I was looking forward to ringing in 1985—a new year, new hope, new promise. Little did I know how life-altering that night would be.

I spent December 31, 1984, moving into an apartment in north Etobicoke with my youngest brother Markel and his girl-friend. I had finished teacher's college that spring and moved to Toronto after graduation. An old friend of mine from Sudbury, who was living in Ottawa, called me up in the afternoon and said, "Karl, I'm having a rough time right now. What are you doing tonight?" My friend Keith was having a New Year's Eve party, so I said, "Come down to Toronto and we'll go to the party together."

Keith's apartment was in North York, at Jane and Lawrence. He was from Trinidad and I'd met him at Lakehead. A winter storm crept in that day, blowing snow across the roads as the temperature plummeted. We arrived at the party, enjoying the warmth of being indoors and the welcoming embrace of my friends. We were having a good time as more people arrived. Later in the evening came another knock at the door. Keith answered and I remember his exact words: "Hey, foxy lady. Come on in." Maria Brand had arrived.

Maria hadn't planned on coming to this party, because she wanted to go to another one. Maria, you see, had major expectations for this particular New Year's Eve. Before leaving her home, she told her friend Olive, "I am going to meet my husband tonight." I'm not sure where Maria had planned to meet her future husband that New Year's Eve, but it wasn't at the party Olive wanted to go to. Maria knew the crowd and did not want to spend her time there. What she did not know was that her future husband was, in fact, among the guests. In life we often know what we want but don't always know where we will find it.

Maria, being a good friend, did what good friends do. She pushed her feelings and needs aside for Olive and agreed to check out the scene at Keith's place.

My plan for the night was less monumental. I just wanted to relax after a hard day of moving. But once Maria arrived I had a hard time looking away. She had dressed up for New Year's Eve and looked nice, with tall winter boots and a form-fitting jacket that accentuated her lovely figure. Then Keith took her coat, revealing a blue silk dress that completely hijacked my attention.

Suddenly, something else was competing for my attention. My stomach. It started to growl. I was hungry but the food hadn't come out yet, so I gravitated toward the popcorn bowl. I wanted to approach Maria, but I was nervous. And when I'm nervous, I eat. Maria couldn't help but notice my repeated trips to the popcorn bowl. Finally, she asked me, "Why are you eating so much popcorn?" That was the icebreaker that got us talking.

Maria and I spent the evening getting to know each other. When it was time to leave, around four in the morning, I literally picked her up and carried her to her car, over the icy sidewalks and snowbanks. It was slippery, and I didn't want her walking to her car.

I also didn't want it to end there. I asked to escort her home, but she said no. I tried to convince her but she held firm. Maria did reward my persistence, however, by inviting me to a New Year's Day party. So 1985 was off to an auspicious start. I picked her up later that day and took her to another party—and we never looked back.

What immediately attracted me to Maria was simple: she reminded me of my mom. No, I wasn't suffering from an Oedipus complex, but my mom was a big part of my life and Maria shared many of her characteristics, such as her appearance, her patience, her sense of humour and her love of cooking. But more importantly, we became good friends; she was someone I could have a conversation with. That was how it was with my mom as well. Before she passed away, I would talk to my mom almost every day.

I believe people use their head, heart and gut to influence decision-making. Rational thinking is using your head in a logical manner. Decisions around emotions are driven by your heart. The feeling in your gut is intuition. I have always trusted it, especially when I met Maria. It told me that she would be right for me.

At the time, Maria was living in an apartment on Greentree Court, which happened to be near the City of York's Board of Education office at 2 Trethewey Drive. I spent more and more time at Maria's apartment. Maria would cook me the best meals, and since I was always hungry, it made for a great situation for my belly and my heart. By the time a year had passed, I had gradually abandoned Markel and moved in full-time with Maria—an arrangement I knew would be forever.

Maria

Maria and I shared a great connection, and we were also on the same page about what we wanted in life. One of the things I wanted, other than to find a teaching job, was to have kids. I had recently finished university and I felt it was time to settle down. The party was over; it was time to get a job and have a family. And after a year of dating, it was also time to start planning a wedding.

Saturday, July 5, 1986, was the exact opposite of the day Maria and I met, a year and a half earlier. Instead of polar winds blowing snow across the road, a cloudy sky and humidity that wrapped around you like a hot, wet blanket marked our gathering. I was dressed and ready to meet Maria at St. Anne's Anglican Church in Toronto. Our apartment was hot, and sweat gathered on my forehead and dripped down my back. I called Maria, who had spent the night at her sister's home north of Toronto in Vaughan, to see if she was ready. She was not ready. We had respected the custom of the bride and groom not seeing each other on the eve of their wedding day.

Finally, Maria was on the road with her driver and brother, Livingston. He was driving his baby sister to the church in a baby-blue Cadillac. It was an older car, and I prayed it would make it all the way to the front steps of the church. My prayers were answered when the car, decorated with streamers and pom-poms, pulled into view. As they drove to the church, other drivers honked their horns, but Livingston's horn was working only sporadically. The lateness, the malfunctioning horn, the hot car with no air conditioning—none of it could stop Maria from smiling. The magic of her wedding day, those feelings of overflowing joy, happiness and anticipation, were all that mattered.

My mom, Fay, had her hands all over the event, from baking and decorating the cakes to cooking food to sewing the wedding dress, which needed some last-minute alterations. Maria's off-white wedding gown resembled a snow-covered mountain, and it played with my imagination and enslaved my eyes. A long, frilly train trailed behind her—a fine display of my mom's skills as a designer and seamstress.

We were an hour behind our 3 p.m. launch time, but the wedding ceremony went smoothly and our guests couldn't wait to get started on the home-cooked wedding feast served in the church hall. All of the food was prepared by our families. We had approximately four hundred guests to feed and entertain. The only people we hired were the photographer and the DJ. The skies may have been overcast, but all the smiles around us were enough to brighten the day and make our photos beautiful. Family and friends stepped up and made our wedding day a success. Not everything went off without a hitch, but we weathered the ups and downs—just as we have continued to do during our life together.

Maria's apartment was a one-bedroom and it became smaller after our wedding as we were given more gifts than cash. We stored boxes of gifts in the living room/dining room area. We couldn't wait to move. We looked at two-bedroom apartments in the area, but Maria, who was working as a mortgage officer for the Canadian Imperial Bank of Commerce, calculated the rent payments would be equal to mortgage payments on a starter home. Why not own and make our money work for us instead of giving it to someone else? So, within months of our wedding, we'd saved enough money to buy a small house in Brampton. We sold it after a year for a tidy profit and moved into a bigger home.

I'm glad Maria is good with our money, because she reminded me recently about something I said when we first met: "I'd rather have a house full of kids than a bankbook full of money." Talk about a self-fulfilling prophecy.

We never talked about how many kids we wanted. One thing I always knew was that I loved kids. I figured if I loved teaching them, working with them and coaching them, I would love having them too. I knew one would not be enough, and I knew I could never have as many as I'd like—say, ten or twelve—which is one reason I became an educator. I used to say to my students, "While you are here at my school, I am your mother and father."

When it comes to parenting, people always say to enjoy the moments, because children grow up in a flash. That's what it seemed like to us. Before you knew it, we were blessed with five kids—our starting five, as I like to call them.

Of course, we didn't have five children at once, our family started with our two daughters. Nastassia and Natasha were good friends, as well as good sisters. Taz was three when Tasha was born, and she admits she was jealous. "I wailed when my mom brought her in the car," she recalls. "I wailed to the point they had to pull off from the highway and take her out. I stopped crying, but then they put her back in and I started wailing again. So I wasn't very kind to new people. I was first-born—what are you going to do?"

Taz soon got used to the new arrival—I don't remember a quarrel between them. Taz was quiet like a mouse while Tasha was like hockey's fourth line, defined by her high energy and rock 'em, sock 'em personality. If you couldn't see her, you could probably hear her singing her favourite song, "Have You Ever Seen the Girl?" She wrote it and performed it whenever we were willing to listen. Taz loved reading, and you would catch her doing it in a quiet corner. We supplied her with dozens of Goosebumps books. Tasha loved her dolls and loved to draw. Both girls started to do the things they enjoyed at an early age, and started to learn what they were good at. School time, sports time and their time made up their daily routines.

Skating and playing basketball were two activities I enjoyed, and I did both with the girls. These were not part-time activities; we would do them up to four times a week. My dream for them was to be good at something other than school. I wanted them to be good skaters and to be good at playing basketball.

The Subban household was obviously a less chaotic place to raise our daughters before our hockey-playing sons arrived over a six-year span.

"Life was good," Taz remembers of her time before the boys arrived. "Every Friday we would go to this restaurant called Shanghai on Old Weston Road and Denison. We called it Fast-Food Fridays. After the boys came, Fast-Food Fridays turned into Home Fridays. That's what I remember—everything got crazier."

Pernell Karl was born in 1989, and as soon as he was old enough to catch a ball he was learning to catch with me. As soon as he was old enough to stand, balance and kick a ball, he was learning to do so with me. The ball was usually a beach ball, because it was colourful, big and soft. He was eager to learn his numbers and letters too. Having two older sisters meant he had two extra teachers. Being the baby in the family made him the centre of attention. He wanted to do everything the adults and his siblings were doing, and there were plenty of hands around to keep him safe, to push him and to encourage him.

The girls were pretty much skating independently when P.K. started skating at around two and a half years old. We spent a couple of back-breaking days holding him so he would learn to balance his body on the thin metal edge of his skate blades, but then he was ready to go on his own. Like the girls, he conquered the liquorice-legs phase quite quickly. Once he moved into the wooden-leg phase, he was ready to take off on his own. I can still see P.K. clamouring for my attention: "Daddy, look what I can do." The more you skate, the better you get. P.K. was getting better and he knew it, and he was proud to share it with me.

By the time Malcolm was born in 1993 and Jordan in 1995, we had sold our second house in Brampton and moved to a four-bedroom home in a recently built subdivision in the Rexdale neighbourhood of north Etobicoke. When we first looked at the house, I said to Maria, "We can't afford it," and I stayed in the car. Maria finally convinced me to go in—and the next thing I knew, we were signing the mortgage papers. Years later, we were glad we'd bought there; it was close to York University and we didn't have enough money for Taz to go out of town for school. Besides being close to York, there were several hockey rinks nearby, which made it a great spot for hockey. Today, Taz and her husband, Andre, are raising their three boys in that house. It's hard to let go of it because of the many memories it holds.

Team Subban

As the family grew, the dynamics changed, and Taz and Tasha took on more responsibilities, often acting like extra parents.

"I did a lot of babysitting. It was a lot of work," Taz says. "Malcolm and Jordan came, basically, back to back. But I don't remember it being a burden. There were also lots of dishes. The girls got the brunt of cleaning and cooking and stuff like that."

Later, when Taz was at York and earning her teaching degree, she was in a position to buy her first car. "I was thinking I'd get a Toyota Camry, but, no, I couldn't put a hockey bag in there, so I bought an SUV so I could drive my brothers to hockey. I needed to help my dad out. There were three boys and three different arenas and my mom didn't drive at the time. My being able to drive changed everything."

There is no doubt Maria and I appreciate the sacrifices Taz and Tasha made for their brothers—and so do they. For instance, when Jordan played in the prestigious Brick Invitational Tournament in Edmonton, Maria and I couldn't go, so Taz took him. "My sisters always played an important role for us," Jordan says. "Without them, I could say, we wouldn't be as successful as we are."

Maria and I never talked about stopping after five children, but Jordan was our last, mainly because Maria became sick while she was pregnant. The pregnancy was high-risk, and they had to monitor her closely to help manage her persistent high blood pressure.

Maria stopped working early in her pregnancy; she was determined to have a healthy baby. My thinking was in line with what we are told to do while in a plane travelling with a child and the oxygen masks are deployed: take care of yourself first, then the child. While Maria the mom was putting her baby ahead of herself, Maria's own health was first in my mind.

Thanks to the doctors who treated her and to Maria's mind-over-body attitude, Maria won the battle but nearly lost the war. She fell ill at home within two weeks of giving birth to Jordan and had to be admitted to the intensive care unit for about a week, but she slowly recovered. When I look at my wife,

I see a rock made of determination. Through this ordeal, we learned not to take our kids or our health for granted.

One of the things I needed when we had a houseful of kids was a lot of energy. I would start the day with a full tank, but by day's end I was running on fumes, not knowing if I would have enough to make it to the finish line—my bed. The major problem we faced as parents is that the finish line continued to change. We would go to bed for a good night's rest but something invariably would get us up prematurely.

I remember a cold winter night when Malcolm and Jordan could not sleep because they both had chickenpox and were restless because of the itching and fever. Either they couldn't sleep or didn't want to sleep, and their crying made the night and early morning blend together. We tried everything we knew or were told would help make them more comfortable. Nothing worked, including prayer. The last trick up our sleeves was to dress them and take them for a car ride. We were hoping the cold air would make them want to sleep. Other than a few taxicabs we were alone on the road. Would this finally do the trick? Forty minutes later we were back home, the sun peeking over the horizon, and Malcolm and Jordan still wide awake. That day's finish line had moved into tomorrow; that's just how parenting works.

And then there are the times when parenting can swiftly turn from joy to terror. One afternoon, I was downstairs when three-year-old P.K. took a beach ball into Tasha's bedroom. She was six at the time. There were the usual sounds of playing and laughter, but they suddenly turned to screaming, and I rushed upstairs to confront a parent's nightmare: my little girl with blood on her face.

It turned out P.K. had thrown the beach ball up in the air, and it had hit the square glass light shade on the ceiling. I don't know if the shade was loose, or if the ball broke it, but it hit the parquet floor and a shard of glass bounced off the floor and into Tasha's eye.

Taz and P.K. stayed at home while Maria and I drove Tasha to Etobicoke General emergency, which was about a ten-minute drive from our home. My car didn't have flashing lights, but I set out driving it like an ambulance. My heart was pounding, my palms were sweaty and I was thinking the worst. Fearing another accident, I slowed down. All I could think was that Tasha could lose her eye.

The doctors at Etobicoke General said it was serious, and we couldn't help but be alarmed when they put Tasha in an ambulance and took her to SickKids hospital in downtown Toronto. We were told there was a chance she could lose her eye.

It was a stressful time for our family. Tasha, however, was in great hands with the doctors at SickKids, and we had every reason to feel hopeful. Luckily, Tasha needed only one surgery to save the vision in her eye.

The silver lining was that the accident brought Tasha and P.K. together. Going through something together can bring you closer. For example, we often see this in sports when teams rally to make the playoffs. They have that one-for-all-and-all-for-one attitude, persevering and feeling the same pain. This is what happened between P.K. and Natasha. P.K. was like a good teammate pulling for his sister to get better.

While accidents do happen, I still questioned whether I should have been providing better supervision. I don't know what I did with that beach ball, but we didn't have too many balls lying around the house after that, and we replaced all the pointy-edged light shades. Tasha was fitted with a pair of glasses, which she embraced, and eventually the scars disappeared and her eye healed completely. But as a parent, the worrying never stops. We hope and pray for the best for our children, but we never know if another crisis is hiding in the weeds.

Six years later, Tasha suffered another serious injury, this time while I was supervising them. And, again, it happened while she was playing with P.K. As Tasha recounts, "P.K. and I would do the stupidest things because we were always in competition, but I always ended up getting hurt."

When Tasha was twelve and P.K nine, I had them working out by running hills in a nearby park. After the training they were allowed to play, so Tasha and P.K. decided to go on the swings. Tasha recalls how she and P.K. were swinging to see who could go higher. "I was way up high, like ten feet in the air, and the seat just snapped and I fell. Free fall. The bottom of the sandbox was metal, and I fell on that metal."

The injury was serious enough that we had to call an ambulance to take Tasha to the hospital. Thankfully, we were able to take her home that night, but the injury essentially ended Tasha's emerging basketball career, and she still suffers from recurring lower back pain.

Based on assumptions and impressions gathered over thirty years as a parent, teacher and principal, I have come to believe that parenting styles fall into three broad categories, with some overlap between approaches. Parenting is a dynamic process; our children are always changing—physically, emotionally, socially and intellectually. The minute you think you have them figured out, they change.

One style of parenting is "autopilot." With this style, children don't have a lot of structure, supervision or role models. Their parents are absent for a large amount of time. Without that guiding force, the kids spend most of their time with their peers and easily pick up negative influences. Coaches, teachers and community groups can work to fill the void, but progress and successes are hard to secure and maintain. These children have a difficult time getting off the ground because of the people around them dragging them down. They often have a tremendous amount of anger, and that anger gets unloaded on society. The adults working with these children are always battling the emotional force field surrounding them.

The second style is "designer parenting." Designer parents have it all figured out. And because they are such perfect parents, their kids can do no wrong. Designer kids have been raised to focus their energy on pleasing Mom, Dad, coaches and teachers. They grow up in the box that their parents designed for them and they conform to all the rules. They know how to make excuses and participate in the blame game. But I say there's a reason why the smaller word *lame* can be found in *blame*: the blame game makes your kid weaker, not stronger. Designer clothes are made to fit you the right way—or perfectly. Designer parents feel it is their job to perfectly design each step their children take on the way to the top. Coaches and teachers are seen as getting in the way of progress. For the most part, these children work solely to please their parents and therefore fail to develop their potential.

The third style is "lifeguard parenting." This is the model Maria and I always tried to espouse. These are the parents who teach their children how to swim and then climb high up on the chair, out of the way. They teach kids how to think for themselves. As children grow—physically, emotionally, intellectually and socially—these parents move slowly and gradually out of the way. They sit off at a distance, yet are always ready to assist: a GPS when children need direction, a doctor when they're not feeling great, a banker when they need money and a police officer when they get "out of hand." I knew my own parents did not want me to be a follower. They wanted me to be courageous enough to make a new road or take the one less travelled. Lifeguard parents see the potential in their children and create an environment that enables them to see it too. The lifeguard's children learn to swim in any water—rough, fast, shallow, dirty or deep.

If you compare raising children to running a business, then it can be said I had the best business partner in Maria. This business had a vision, a mission and an action plan. We knew our roles and we did not get in each other's way. Maria was supportive of me but never hesitated to express her feelings or to impose her will if she felt I was not acting in the best interest of the children. For example, when Taz or P.K. refused to do their drills in the basement it would make me miserable, which affected my relationship with them. Maria would say the right things to them and, with a hug, make it all better.

TAZ

"In terms of goals, both of them wanted us do well in school, get a career, work your hardest at everything you do. Dad was more the person to implement that and Mom was more about making sure you have clean clothes, making sure you have eaten, making sure you were okay mentally. Dad was the one to push you to do the physical work. He'd say, 'Okay, we are going outside to do sprints now and do your thousand skips a day.' Our basement wasn't finished, and Dad would have us down there doing dribbling drills, skipping, push-ups—all that stuff. They were both pretty similar in stressing that if you're going to do something just do it 100 percent or don't bother doing it at all.

"[After a game] Mom was more the person to say, 'Oh, way to go.' Dad would say, 'You played okay but you didn't get five rebounds you should have gotten, you didn't do this, you didn't do that.' I found that for P.K., that style worked, the critical analysis of the game. For me, it worked up to a certain point, then I realized I couldn't take this anymore. I basically tuned out. P.K. was able to take that because I think his personality is different. And Malcolm and Jordan pretty much take it too. He wasn't trying to be mean, it was more of a matter of, 'I want you to get better, so this is what we are doing.' He could see all those things. My mom was more of the encourager. They balanced each other."

JORDAN

"Your mother is always easy to talk to. My dad was always trying give me advice and make me better. My mom said, 'Jordan, just do what you love.' My mom was just . . . a little softer, not as hard on me. They were both always very thoughtful, very positive and encouraging. They set me straight when I needed to be set straight, as well."

P.K.

"There were times where my dad was taking the hard-nose approach and my mom was taking the other one, and then there were times when my mom was taking the hard approach and my dad was taking the softer approach. So they were very good in terms of working together. There were a lot of times where they disagreed, where one thought maybe they needed to be harder and the other person thought, 'Hey listen, back off a little bit.'

"But there's no perfect way to coach a child or to comfort your child. I think the more adversity your son or daughter goes through the better it's going to be for them, and the one thing that has allowed me to have success in my life, through my career, is that whenever somebody's taken a shot at me, or tried to knock me down, I've always persevered, and that's from the experiences of playing hockey growing up. My parents never babied me in those moments, they never stood out there to hold my hand. They said, 'Listen, at the end of the day you need to stand up and be accountable. If you're the player that you say you are then go out and show it.'"

We spent a lot of time with our children. The person you spend the most time with influences you the most, and Maria and I both wanted to be that influencer. You also have to make sure you love them unconditionally. Children need your love and your emotional support. When they know you care, they will care about what you have to say to them. If you care, you'll also discipline them, and you'll provide them with the resources they need to succeed. Those prerequisites must be there in order for them to succeed. If those prerequisites were not there, our daughters would not have spent hours doing basketball drills or running hills, and our sons would not have shot the pucks in the basement. And Daddy was also there with them. You must never underestimate this. It's not that P.K. loved hockey so much or my grandkids love skating so much. What they loved—and I'll debate this with anyone—is the time they spent with Maria and me.

Discipline is a function, sometimes, of how you were raised. I was raised in Jamaica, with its British influence and emphasis on authority, and a certain reliance on corporal punishment. Maria was raised differently. In our house there were all sorts of discipline. There were time outs. There was yelling, and probably things yelled that should not have been yelled. And then there was "the look." When I use it, my kids know exactly what I'm thinking. It still works today.

Maria never liked the heavy-handed stuff, just like my mother. Growing up, I received a few spankings and, for better or worse, my kids did too. P.K. got it a little bit and all the kids would fall in line after that.

Maria and I had our biggest disagreements about discipline when it came to their sports. If a punishment was warranted, Maria would threaten them by saying, "You're not allowed to go to practice" or "You're not going to play your games." I didn't believe in that. Taking away their hockey would have been counterproductive.

In the end, the boys never missed hockey. For me, sending them to their room, denying them TV, making them do extra chores was good enough. Also, part of playing hockey was belonging to a team. If you miss a game or a practice, then you are also letting the team down. When you deny a child piano class or hockey, they could end up wanting to quit altogether. To me, sports are a life changer and sometimes even a lifesaver.

This is why, as a principal, I wasn't the type to take away recess or gym class as punishments.

After five years of marriage, Maria and I had a backyard barbecue to celebrate our anniversary with family and friends.

The five-year mark was an important milestone—one that applies to teaching as well as marriage. If you can survive the first five years of both marriage and teaching, you will do just fine. I have done just fine in both. I retired after thirty years of teaching; my marriage to Maria has no retirement date. It will continue until death do us part. We have made it work and we continue to do so.

What made our marriage work? Love, trust, empathy and an ability to listen are the first things that come to mind. However, the special ingredient for us was raising five children. This big project brought us closer together and kept us working together. Child rearing was either about doing something new or doing something difficult. We needed each other as much as our children needed us to make things work. The time we invested in our children was also time invested in our relationship. Quality "people time" leads to healthy relationships and a healthy marriage. I knew I could count on Maria and she knew she could count on me, especially when the going was tough. We worked around the clock and made it looked routine. We were the two coaches of Team Subban, and we're still happy to share those duties.

We did not always agree on everything, but we never lost sight of the most important thing in our lives—our children. So far, we had been up to all the challenges we'd faced early on in our marriage and parenting lives. We were building a solid foundation, which was critical if we were going to survive the biggest test of our resiliency, a test that would dominate our lives for years to come. It was waiting just around the corner.

Minor Hockey

It was a Friday night and I had the hockey bag open on the living room floor. I was taking out the hockey equipment—some of it new, some of it used—donated to P.K. by two of my colleagues, Barb Smales and David Bince. P.K. was four years old. He was sitting on the couch, barely able to contain his excitement. It was the night before his first hockey game ever, with the Flames in the Chris Tonks Arena house league program. I had no idea what I was doing.

When I took all the crazy-looking pieces out of the bag for the dry run, it was like putting together a puzzle without the picture on the box. I was lost, and, unfortunately, YouTube tutorials had yet to be invented. The garter belt mystified me completely, and the straps for the shoulder pads were another problem. I got part of the puzzle solved that night and the rest of it the next morning at the arena where I could steal a glance at how it was done in the dressing room.

For the first few games, I got P.K. dressed at home because I didn't want to be embarrassed at the arena. It was like learning to drive a car: I was nervous at first, but I got the hang of it and soon enough it became second nature. Not only was P.K. learning a new game, but I was learning a game too: how kids were coached in minor hockey—which could contrast quite a bit with how we were taught to teach kids in the education system.

On that first house league team, P.K. was playing with kids who were two to three years older than him. He didn't look out of place. At four years old, P.K. was already a good skater. Maybe he didn't have an understanding of the game because of his age, but he could keep up and he could carry the puck and make moves with it. Once, he did take the puck to the wrong net—briefly earning the nickname Wrong Way—but overall he had a lot of success that year, and I was encouraged by the progress I saw on the ice.

A key component of the success our daughters and sons have experienced was the value we placed on practice. Practice mattered more to me than games. I realize now that one of the best gifts I gave Taz, Tasha, P.K., Malcolm and Jordan is helping them be good at something at a young age. It builds self-confidence.

The next year, we took P.K. to Pine Point Arena in Etobicoke, where he was the talk of house league. The year he turned five, he was on the six-year-old all-star team. That year, the team scored twenty-one goals, and P.K. netted nineteen of them. A lot of people questioned his age. He was big and looked bigger because I always bought him equipment he could grow into (and that his brothers would later inherit). When he was six, we took him out of house league and brought him to the West Mall Lightning, a select team. He was playing with the Super 8s, the all-star team for eight-year-olds. We didn't find out until the end of the season that he was not allowed to play two years ahead.

The seed of my sons playing hockey was planted when I was a teenager in Sudbury. Even though I never played on a real team, I always saw my sons pursuing the hockey dream I couldn't. It started with watching *Hockey Night in Canada* and skating together as a family.

The children were not forced to watch hockey. P.K. was all energy in those days and couldn't sit still. With me cheering or yelling at the television, he would run over, jump on me or sit beside me, yelling or screaming at the television like he knew what was going on. The kids became fans of the game because Maria and I were fans of the game. Maria supported the Toronto Maple Leafs because she grew up in Toronto. When the Habs and Leafs played, one of us would have bragging rights until they played each other again. Hockey injected fun, joy and laughter into our family life. So by the time P.K. said to me—while we were watching the Montreal Canadiens playing on a Saturday night—"Daddy, I want to play hockey like those guys on TV," he was already immersed in the sport.

Learning to skate is perhaps the most important ingredient in becoming a good hockey player. Skating as a family was as routine to us as eating family dinners. It was our main family activity during the winter months, and we skated on many different ice surfaces around the Greater Toronto Area.

When we lived in Brampton, one of our favourite places to go was Bramalea City Centre. I'll never forget one particular family outing. We pulled into the parking lot of the outdoor public rink on a Friday night. Betsy, my 1983 Toyota Corolla, was just big enough for four people, but by that time we had an extra passenger: P.K. He was two that spring, about to turn three. P.K. was flanked by his sisters in the backseat, and Maria, my co-pilot, joined me in the front. She had the hot chocolate in a Thermos with Styrofoam cups in a plastic bag at her feet. The parking lot, usually full of cars, was empty, so I was able to park close to the rink. On most Friday evenings, the place was packed with teenagers and families with young children, blades carving the ice surface as music pounded from the outdoor speakers.

On this night, though, the rink was quiet. A cold weather alert was in effect, warning the good citizens of the Greater Toronto Area to avoid outdoor activities because of the potential health hazard, especially to children. When it's this bitterly cold, you don't want to move. It feels as if the cold is sticking to your body. Sitting on the concrete bench to put on skates was painful, especially for me, wearing sweatpants. Our routine was that the kids would sit beside me with their closest leg on my lap. I would lace up that skate, then move to do the other one. I would even tie Maria's skates, until she fell one day and sprained her wrist. That marked her official retirement from skating.

On the Friday night in question, Taz, Natasha and P.K. were wearing snowsuits, and were well protected from the wind chill. But by the time I completed looping everybody's laces, my fingers were numb. I cupped my hands to my mouth and tried blowing warm air on my aching fingers. They worked enough to tighten my skates and start the slow merry-go-round. We didn't last very long that night, but we certainly earned and appreciated our hot chocolate treat afterwards.

Once the cold weather settles in, the reflecting pool at Nathan Phillips Square, at the foot of the curved towers of Toronto City Hall, becomes an outdoor rink. It is among the first outdoor skating surfaces to open each season, an occasion that marks the unofficial start of winter in the city.

Even though P.K. was an above-average skater for his age, I wasn't satisfied with his ability. I knew that the more he did it, the better he'd become. The winter he was in senior kindergarten, 1994–95, the goal for P.K. was to skate every day—and the earlier in the season that started, the better. That meant hitting Nathan Phillips Square at 10 p.m.

I would have preferred driving downtown earlier in the evening to skate, but my job made that impossible. I had applied for a vice-principal position at Runnymede Collegiate's adult night school program. It started at 6 p.m. and lasted until around 9 p.m. I needed the experience as a vice-principal because I was working toward becoming an elementary principal. On those weeknights, I would leave school between 9 p.m. and 9:30 p.m., drive home, change, then wake up P.K., who had gone to bed wearing his snowsuit. Then we'd get in the car and drive downtown.

Public skating would end around 10 p.m., and the crowd would slowly thin out, gradually ceding the space to the shinny players, who would stride onto the ice with sticks in hand. Soon they would outnumber the pleasure skaters, and in no time P.K. would be in the middle of the ice, on his knees, carrying out the shinny ritual of picking sides. All the sticks were thrown into a pile, and P.K. loved to pull them out one at a time to make the teams. The shinny spirit was on full display, with the older players passing the puck to the kids and letting them score.

I never played at Nathan Phillips Square, but I'd walk around the rectangular rink watching P.K. and thinking about how hockey was making him feel the way it had made me feel as a kid growing up on Peter Street in Sudbury. He'd been bitten by the hockey bug, and he saw himself as one of the players. The tourists also enjoyed seeing this little black boy skating late at night with the adults. We'd stay until one or two in the morning, then get a slice of pizza and go home. There wasn't full-day kindergarten at the time, and P.K. attended the afternoon class, so he could sleep in the next day. We carried out this ritual every night for two or three weeks until the city rinks in North Etobicoke opened, meaning we didn't have to go all the way downtown to get P.K.'s skating practice in.

When you feed a dream, you make it stronger and more likely to happen. That is what Maria and I did as parents. We watched games together on television and made time to be with our children as they practised, trained and played. Over time, I realized the importance of not only feeding the hockey dream but also building those life skills associated with being a good person.

The hockey lesson plan for the boys focused on four activities: skating, shooting pucks, stick handling and playing shinny. These activities were loaded into their GPS, and we did them year round. My boys had the most fun during the shinny games. Shinny was like their favourite dessert: they couldn't wait to have it and could never get enough. During the winter months, shinny was played mostly on the outdoor rink at Sunnylea Park in Etobicoke. The boys wouldn't stop playing until all the rink rats called it a day—or night. I would always have a Thermos of hot chocolate waiting, with cups for each of them. The boys were never cold because they were always moving, and they would end up shedding layers of clothing as competition raised their body temperature.

I was always there when the boys were on the shinny ice. When Malcolm and Jordan were learning to skate, I would skate with them on the perimeter while P.K. played in the middle with the older boys. As soon as Malcolm and Jordan were ready to participate in the shinny games, I was like a lifeguard sitting in the distance. I never had to come in and rescue them; the older boys looked out for the younger ones. Unlike in their organized hockey games, adult interference was never seen or heard. There were no referees, linesmen, goal judges, fans or scorekeeper, and no one was benched. This was hockey in its purest form, kids playing because it was fun.

Children love to play. That's how they spend the majority of their waking hours. Starving young children of the opportunity to play is denying them a rite of passage. Maria and I took full advantage of our daughters' love for basketball and our sons' passion for hockey as a tool not only to teach them the importance of being good at something but also to grow life skills. Hockey skills make you a good hockey player; life skills make you productive, happier and healthier over your lifetime.

———

In 1993, we moved to Arborwood Drive in the north Etobicoke neighbourhood known as Rexdale, near Woodbine Racetrack. Our house had four bedrooms and a big backyard. We didn't pay a million dollars for it, but it was worth a million bucks to us. More than just a roof over our heads, it was a place where our family ethic of working, learning and playing could thrive. The saying that the home is the first school and parents the first teachers was made for us. Malcolm and Jordan were born while we were in Rexdale.

Our home was very lived in, and rich with things to do. The moment you walked in the door you saw toys, hockey sticks and mini nets scattered here and there. The house was set up like a kindergarten classroom, with a number of learning or activity centres. There were plenty of books, and when the kids were too young to read independently, we had cassette tapes and books on computer for them to read and follow along. There was an assortment of physical education equipment and a piano in our living room. Taz and Tasha took piano lessons from a teacher who lived next door. The boys did not take formal lessons, but learned to play it too. It was just as easy to pick up a hockey stick as it was to sit at the piano and bang out some noise. They could always find paper, pencils or crayons to draw or colour. A favourite activity was making kites from bamboo sticks, glue and coloured tissue paper. Independent play was important, and we never forced one activity over the other.

Being an educator, I got to spend my summers with the kids. This was when we would cook together. I loved baking, and they loved measuring the ingredients for cakes. Another favourite was Easter buns, which I've been making for more than twenty-five years, from a recipe I saved from the *Toronto Star*.

The backyard on Arborwood Drive served three main purposes. First, it was a safe place for our children to play during the warm weather seasons. Second, it housed our grapevines, Bing cherry and pear trees, and my vegetable garden. That garden was about five feet deep and ran the width of the backyard. I love to plant and see things grow. And I love to share my harvest.

The third purpose it served was for skating. For about fifteen years, the backyard rink was part of my winter routine. A fellow teacher, Don Norman, inspired me—he built outdoor rinks at his school, Harwood Public, and at his house. Don gave me the basic recipe, but I took it a bit further by using a tarp and boards. I saw an ad for a tarp, I think in *The Hockey News,* and sent away for one.

Making the thirty-by-thirty-foot rink was a test of my patience, resilience and ability to work hard. The easy part of the process is nailing or joining the boards together and putting the rink tarp in place. Once the tarp is laid, water is run on the surface to keep the tarp down and in position for the deep freeze. Sometimes winter came before Christmas, and I was able to make a solid base, but one or two days of above-zero temperatures would bring me back to the starting line.

Starting over is something you have to get used to when you're making a backyard rink. There are no guarantees when it comes to the weather. You need consistent cold temperatures and a certain amount of snowfall. Progress is always slow, so it can be difficult to see. Wetting the surface a little bit each day is the key. Sometimes I would get up at 3 a.m.; that's when it's the coldest, and therefore the best time to spray the surface.

P.K. on the backyard rink

The Subban backyard rink allowed the boys to skate every day and develop a skating ability that separated them from most players their age. It was their job to skate and my job to maintain the skating surface. If it became too warm, I would shovel snow on the surface to protect it from the heat of the sun.

The other problem I encountered with the rink concerned my neighbour. The rink tarp developed a few leaks over the years, and water would escape into his backyard. Overnight the water froze, resulting in an unwanted ice surface for him. He told Maria I should stop making the rink because one day he was going to break his neck while taking out his garbage. I tried patching the tarp but it didn't work; I had to buy a new one from Home Depot. That first tarp lasted about ten years.

Whenever my backyard rink was out of commission, I would take the boys to a city rink. I knew the skating schedule for every rink around Toronto and Mississauga. Distance was no deterrent—if it was open for public or family skating, we were there.

One thing I learned in those years—and I believe this applies to all parents—is that it's important not to use other people's kids as a measuring stick. You are setting your own standard. I've always said that the time and energy I spend focusing on somebody else's kid is time and energy I could be using to help my own child to be better.

If I was tired, or the kids were sick, we might have only ten minutes to skate, so that is what we'd do. That was our mindset all along—to be better. I tried to teach my students the same way. You work to get better, not to get As. Otherwise, once you get As, why would you keep working? Never mind the letter—you can always be better.

Malcolm and Jordan followed P.K. into organized hockey. They got their start with the Etobicoke Bulldogs Hockey Association. All three joined house league around age four.

To me, house league hockey is like kindergarten. Everything is new. Your coach is like your first teacher. Teammates are like classmates. There is new equipment and a uniform to learn and use. There are rules and routines to learn and follow. And some children start kindergarten ahead of their classmates, having been exposed to a rich and stimulating environment at home during their first five years.

Like those children who get off to a good start in kindergarten, all of my boys found success in house league. Playing, practising and training in hockey was routine for them by their fifth birthday. The house leagues were made up of teams, and each team organized its players into A, B and C lines. The A line was the top group, B was the average group and C was for those players who could barely stand on their skates. From year one, P.K., Malcolm and Jordan played only on the A line, already able to skate and carry the puck.

MARIA

My kids grew to like the sport because they were good at it. When people say, "My kids don't like this, they don't like that," my answer is the parents have to devote the time to it. Hockey takes a big commitment. A lot of parents don't want to do it.

Money is another thing, but you really don't spend a lot of money until they play AAA and there is a lot of travelling, with hotel costs. In minor hockey, take them once a week to a game and to practice. People think you have to have them in power skating. No, take them public skating every day. Take your book and read while the kid goes skating. It is only going to make their skating better. When they really skate well, then put them into power skating. Parents get the wrong concept. They want to do everything at once and then put a lot of pressure on their kids.

P.K. started power skating at six, but he was that good a skater. He used to hate it. He used to hate getting up Sunday mornings. He used to cry. I said, "If you want to play the game and you want to get better, you have to go to power skating. You don't want to get better, you don't have to go." I tell them like it is. "If you want to go to the NHL, like you say, then you have to go to power skating, so make up your mind." I said it that way. Karl used to say, "You're going!"

The games were played on Saturday mornings, and to this day I can still smell the peameal bacon cooking at Pine Point

Arena. We all looked forward to a bacon sandwich after the games. The family who cooked the bacon owned a butcher shop, and they would set up a kiosk in the front of the arena. The smell of that bacon was the only thing that could momentarily distract me from my sons' hockey games on those Saturday mornings.

I will also always remember the passion displayed by the parents the minute we walked through the arena door. It reminded me of the first day of school after summer holidays, when super-charged students returned with energy and anticipation. Parents and young kids would be cheering, yelling, shouting and hollering throughout the hockey games, and with the spirit of competition in the mix, it made it very easy for adults to get lost in the moment.

"Shoot it! Dump it! Skate! Skate! Focus! Focus!"

Loud cheers for goals and wins and silence for goals against and losses defined the rhythm for each game. I wasn't a yeller or screamer. I spent many hours videotaping the boys, not to use as a teaching tool, but strictly for the memories. When you watch the hundreds of hours of game tape, I am very quiet, but you can hear Maria yelling encouragement to all of the players, not just her sons.

I may not have always displayed my emotion in the stands, but it came out in other ways. One winter, P.K. was very sick with the flu on a game day. My head—along with Maria's voice—told me he should not play, but my heart said he should. All morning I looked for signs he was getting better, but P.K., remained in the clutches of a high temperature and displayed little energy.

I dressed P.K. under protest from Maria, and he played that morning to please me. But as I watched my sick and lethargic son trying to skate, I realized I'd made a big mistake. Frankly, I was embarrassed.

Afterwards, I apologized to Maria, though regrettably not to P.K., and vowed not to repeat this mistake. I was reminded of my golden rule of working with children: always make decisions that are in the best interest of the child and the child's health. To this day, when I start to blow my own horn about my great parenting moves, Maria will bring me back to earth by reminding me of the decision I made that Saturday morning.

My greatest challenge during those minor hockey years was capping my emotions after the games. Whenever the boys' teams lost, I felt I'd lost too. When they won their game on Saturday, I felt great for the week. It was this roller coaster of emotions that triggered P.K.'s coach, Coach Richard, to tell the parents of the six-year-old all-star team (P.K. was five at the time) to take better care of ourselves or we were not going to make it through the minor hockey years. He was right. We could not continue the way we were going, using up so much energy agonizing over winning or losing. I always felt hockey brought out the best in us—and sometimes the worst.

Coach Richard dispensed other valuable advice. He told parents during a team meeting that the coaches did not recognize superstars. He didn't single out any one of us, but P.K. was their best skater and scorer, and I left the meeting feeling that Coach Richard was saying to me, "Karl, P.K. doesn't need to feel at age five that he is a superstar." He was so right. We learned over the years that the goal of hockey parenting was not making superstars, it was making better hockey players.

For a hockey team to win, kids have to do certain things on the ice, but one of the things I learned is they are not always ready intellectually, socially, physically or emotionally to do the things we want them to do on any given day. When P.K., Malcolm and Jordan started hockey, they could skate well and they could stickhandle, but they weren't always ready to go into the pack where the puck was. I had to have faith that the necessary skills would come over time, as each boy developed at his own pace.

I learned from teaching that kids go through different stages of development and have different characteristics. The younger they are the more concrete they are in their thinking. As they get older, they transition into a more formal type of thinking. The minute I was able to translate this knowledge to hockey, I realized I needed to just let go and enjoy the ride. Have fun. I learned this lesson with P.K., and by the time Malcolm and Jordan came along I wasn't so intense. With P.K. being the first, his hockey took a lot of our energy.

It also took time. Our lives were divided into three parts: home time, sports time and work/school time. Sports time was the most demanding and challenging. Three boys playing and practising hockey all over the city and two girls playing rep basketball meant Saturdays and Sundays were always blur. We missed some of the girls' games because we would drop them off and then pick up them up later. When the girls became older we were comfortable with them being driven by other parents or taking public transit, often with their teammates. For many years we had only one car. It was only when Taz started at York University that we got a second vehicle, and she helped out by taking her brothers to practices and games.

Sometimes I would ask my friend Dave Bince to help out. One Saturday, he drove P.K. to his house league game. P.K. got lost in the conversation and, without looking at Dave, called him "Dad." After that, Dave would joke with me that P.K. had two dads. It never bothered me; I knew it would take a village to raise my children, and a village to raise National Hockey League players.

I never believed in bribing my children to get them to achieve. But that didn't stop others, such as my mother's brother, Uncle Owen. He was visiting us from Sudbury on a day when P.K. was about to play a house league game at Pine Point Arena. Before we walked out the door, Uncle Owen took a five-dollar bill out of his pocket and waved it in the air, saying to P.K., with a big smile on his face, "You will get one of these for each goal you score today."

Maria and I considered this kind of outright bribery a no-no, but we let it go this time. My uncle was not with us every day, and we did not feel this one-time event would have a lasting effect on our son's motivation. P.K., of course, had a great game. He scored five goals and couldn't wait to collect from Uncle Owen.

On the drive home, I took advantage of this meaningful math moment. We spent the fifteen-minute car ride counting by fives. Uncle Owen learned something too—that was the last time he offered money to P.K., or his brothers, to score goals.

There are two types of motivation—extrinsic and intrinsic. Uncle Owen's transaction with P.K. is an example of extrinsic motivation. When the reward comes from the outside, children lose interest over time and their drive for playing evaporates. Intrinsic motivation comes from within. When you play out of interest, and because it is fun and enjoyable to be with others, you are doing it for yourself. And when you do it for yourself, you do it more and for a longer time, and you get better.

Part of getting better is removing distractions. Even though Maria and I wanted our children to be focused while on the ice and on the bench, our boys always wanted to know where we were sitting or standing in the arena. This was more pronounced during their early years in hockey. To wean them off searching for us in the stands—and reduce their separation anxiety—we would hide from them! It worked. Over time, it didn't matter where Mom and Dad were sitting. The arena, the ice, the puck, referees, fans, teammates and opposing team were not a distraction, and no longer represented the unknown. The goal was for them to be immersed in their hockey, caught up in the feeling of "I am loving this game and I can play this game."

While I think there are many benefits for kids playing sports, Maria and I had strong beliefs about the importance of our sons taking their hockey seriously as they got older. One day, Maria was having lunch with a high-school friend and the conversation turned to their kids playing hockey. When her friend said her kids were playing only to have fun and get exercise, Maria explained how our approach was different: "If they only want to have fun, I will leave them in house league. If they only want exercise, I will give them a gym membership." Playing hockey was expensive, and we wanted a bit more of a return on our investment. We believed the bar you set is the bar they achieve, and you get what you expect. We expected more. A whole lot more.

MARIA

When P.K. was in minor bantam he played for the Senators. I said, "You are fourteen, you are old enough, if they don't want to play you, you know what you have to do. Whatever ice time you get, you just go play. If it's ten seconds, you do something—you go out there and take a hit, or you score a goal, or you make a good pass. You do something, whatever they give you. Just don't go out there and sulk.

Kids have to understand this is the politics of hockey. . . . They are going to play you based on how you play. That's how it is. That's how we got P.K. ready, because when he went to Belleville he was ready for that.

When the coach would sit P.K.'s ass, he knew the next shift he had to be ready to play. The NHL is same thing. So we helped him understand: this is not minor hockey where there are three of you carrying the team and you get all the ice time. At this level you have to be producing to get your ice time.

One day we were at the Vaughan Iceplex in Toronto. It's a double rink that smells musty and mouldy, and the Zamboni engine smokes too much. But that never mattered. It's hockey. You put up with it. I remember it was a spring tournament and P.K. was about eight. He came out of the dressing room crying. He said a boy on the ice called him the N-word.

We had never experienced this before, so we'd never had any conversations about the N-word. My parents had never had that discussion with me, either. This never would have happened in Jamaica, and in Sudbury, they never came home and complained about anyone saying something racially motivated to them. And I had never had anyone say it to me.

Maria and I reacted the same way. We said there was no need to cry because it was only a word. We probably said something about "sticks and stones." There weren't too many kids playing hockey who looked like P.K., so I'm quite sure he knew he was different. But now someone had communicated it to him in a way he didn't like.

The second time something like that came up was in Waterloo, Ontario, at a tournament. P.K. would have been about nine. I walked by a crowd of parents in the stands toward where parents from our team were sitting. Suddenly, I heard a lot of yelling. I looked back and saw one of the parents from our team, the father of a current NHL player, in the middle of the commotion. Somebody had something derogatory about P.K. and this father stepped in to defend him. To this day, he's never told me what was said, but I guess I can imagine.

The message I gave the boys regarding incidents like this evolved over time. It's such a sensitive thing. For me, the younger they learned to deal with these situations the better. Racism is a fact of life. People may not like other people for a variety of reasons: our height, the clothes we wear, our weight—who knows? Everybody's different in some way, and being different doesn't make you defective.

I always told my kids that dealing with racism on a personal level is like many other distractions in life: the minute you pay attention to it, you take your eyes off your destination. You'll never get where you want to go. So why give it permission to distract you?

My feeling is that the best way to deal with racism is to develop your potential. There are people who don't believe in you because of the colour of your skin, so the best way to show them and show the world is to become something.

There are those who don't accept this view. If you want to live by thinking about what those people said to you or what you think they think about you, I can't stop you. But I don't want any part of it. If P.K. had taken the time to take on all the negativity that has been thrown his way, he would not have gotten where he is today. He has always just pushed it aside.

I have been asked, more than once, whether my public point of view on this is different from what I feel privately. It is one thing to project this attitude in front of cameras and microphones, some people suggest, but what about when you are alone? In those quiet moments, can the racist comments sink in? I say no, because it just weighs you down. When the doors are closed, it's the same mindset. I've told P.K. it's vital to just change the channel, because if you ruminate over it, you can't free yourself from it. It does take practice, though—and P.K. has had a lot of opportunities to practise.

The most important belief you have is the belief in yourself. What a wonderful lesson to teach our kids. It (regardless of what negative thing "it" might be) only affects you if you give it permission to affect you. If someone throws a banana on the ice, am I going to stop playing hockey? Come on.

There was a coach when P.K. was young who told him after a tournament that he was never going to make it in hockey. P.K. had two options: believe the coach and stop playing, or carry on. I like to say, "You must go through something to become something," and that means you have to face adversity. Those hard challenges are your exams. If you don't pass them, you are not going to make it. The price you pay is the training you do, the sacrifices you make and the critics you deal with. And there will be many of them—the voices saying you are not fast enough, you are not that good defensively, you lack hockey sense. As I told him one time: "There are three senses you need to understand to make it in hockey: hockey sense, common sense and nonsense. You use your hockey sense on the ice, you use your common sense off the ice and you have to know what to do with the nonsense, because a lot of it is nonsense."

That is the feedback I give to all of my children, because I needed them to deeply understand this when I was no longer their coach and their trainer. I wanted my advice to be the streetlight at night when it's dark and the sunshine that lights their path during the day.

One of my heart-stopping moments in hockey happened in the stands at Beatrice Ice Gardens at York University in Toronto. P.K. was playing for the Mississauga Reps of the GTHL, and they were hosting a team that had a much better record. Leading up to the game, coach Martin Ross told the players and parents that we would be having a special guest drop by. Word got out just before game time that the Montreal Canadiens legend Jean Béliveau was in the players' dressing room, delivering the pre-game talk. How I wanted to be the parent fly on that wall!

The players hit the ice for their customary five-minute pre-game skate. You could feel the energy and the excitement.

Once the game started, Mr. Béliveau was brought over to sit with me. I still can't believe it. He called me Karl, and we talked as if I had known him for years. We talked about P.K., about Jean's playing hockey for the Bleu-Blanc-Rouge and about parenting. He told me that twenty years ago, hockey parents in Quebec were given a green card or a red card. A green card meant you could watch your kid play; a red card meant your behaviour was offside and you had to leave the rink. I was very happy that day to be given a green card to sit with one of hockey's greats.

In the dressing room, Jean Béliveau had told P.K. that as the captain, he plays for his team, and it was his job to help them play better. It was as if Mr. Béliveau injected each player with a shot of adrenaline. The boys didn't look the same or play the way they had been playing before that game, thanks to the magic of Jean Béliveau.

The minor hockey years played a major role in our lives. Those experiences were crucial to my children's hockey development and to our education as hockey parents. The biggest takeaway I have from that time is that hockey matters but people matter more. P.K., Malcolm and Jordan loved playing hockey, but, most importantly, they enjoyed the time hockey made for Mom and Dad to spend with them.

As Maria said, "What hockey does—any sport—it brings parents closer to their kids, because you spend that time you wouldn't otherwise spend. If you just work and come home, oh, you are so tired, you go watch TV. If you go to a game, you spend that time with them, buying hot chocolate, talking about the game; it's a family thing. That is what I love about the sport. It developed that closeness as a family."

And the kids remember those times too. The stories come up, for instance, during the annual mother/son trips the NHL teams organize. "All the boys have to talk about their moms and what made them so special," Maria said. "They remember the days we had to make them dinner. Parents come home and they are tired but they make sure everything is done. I said to P.K., 'You remember that? In the kitchen and rushing to make dinner and then go to the game?' These NHL players are thirty, and they remember all the good things Momma did."

8

The Twenty-Four-Hour Rule

"**P**.K. Let's go!"

Sitting on the bench, my ten-year-old son looked a bit puzzled for a moment, then returned his focus to the game his team was playing.

I repeated my instruction.

"P.K. Let's go!"

It was a tone he knew well. He looked at me again, and I motioned for him to follow me to the dressing room.

"Start taking off your equipment," I said sternly, once we

were behind closed doors. "We're going home. We're done with this team."

A perplexed team official followed us into the dressing room. "What are you doing?" he asked. He was concerned I was making a dire mistake, and anxious to stress that he'd never seen a parent pull a player from a team during a game.

"Well," I said, "you're seeing it now."

"What do we do with the jersey?" P.K. asked.

"We are leaving it right here," I said.

And that was it for us and the Toronto Red Wings, one of the elite minor atom–level AAA teams in the Greater Toronto Hockey League.

In the heat of the moment, I didn't fully realize the impact of the decision I made during that game. Suddenly, P.K. was a kid without a team—and without the opportunity to play elite hockey, his NHL dreams began to slide away, like a puck moving off his stick.

I don't remember which straw broke the camel's back that day; it wasn't so much one thing as the same old thing. Both Maria and I felt P.K.'s growth and development as a player was being hindered, and his self-esteem suffering.

There are a couple of things you can do when you notice a problem: you can leave it alone and see if it goes away, or you can address it if you perceive there's a pattern. Over time, we noticed it wasn't going away.

One example I remember vividly came during a team penalty kill. The coach, Harry Evans, put P.K. on the ice, but when

P.K. had control of the puck, Harry would start yelling, "Rag the puck! Rag the puck!" Ragging the puck is having one player control it, killing off time instead of passing or even trying to score. I sat in the stands, wondering what was going on. Why was the coach demanding P.K. rag the puck? He wasn't doing this with any other players. P.K. would be out there for two or three minutes, and not once would he be told to shoot the puck down the ice, which is what a player should do while killing a penalty. Instead, the coach just kept yelling, "Rag the puck!"

Then P.K. would go to the bench and sit for ten minutes. Players should be on regular shifts of two to three minutes. Teams at this level usually have three lines of players and two centres. The players are rotated. P.K. played centre at the time.

One of the things Maria and I tried not to do was tell coaches how to coach our son. We had made no demands regarding linemates or playing time. And I don't believe in fair ice time. You'd never hear me say, "This player got five minutes of ice time, so P.K. should get five minutes." And yet, I didn't think he should be sitting for what seemed like ten minutes between shifts.

Another problem occurred during practices. Harry and his two assistants would be working on a formation, or a power play, and P.K. wouldn't get a turn. There would be five players in the drill and P.K. would not be one of them. I remember Harry saying to P.K., "Can you just move over there? Let's get somebody else who can put the puck in the net."

I know the world is not fair and that not everyone is treated the same. But we wanted P.K. to feel like he belonged. At ten years old, children are still impressionable. It was P.K.'s job to listen to his coach; that is how he was taught—to be coachable and respectful. But now he was getting mixed messages. We knew he wasn't feeling good about himself because we would talk about it. You know when your child is happy. Each time you go to the rink it should be like going to a birthday party—and it wasn't.

MARIA

Practice is when I first noticed the problems. Karl wasn't at all the practices. They would be running a practice and P.K. would be on the sidelines not doing anything.

Then we were at the game and noticed P.K. wasn't being played. He was just sitting there. He thought he had done something wrong. That's not good for a ten-year-old. He was just sitting there and the coach wasn't saying anything to him. This is minor hockey, not the OHL or the NHL. Kids just want to play. Now, this was early in the season. At the beginning of the season you expect the coach to use everybody. It wasn't happening for P.K. And it wasn't that he was missing a shift here or there. He was just not being played.

During games and practices, Maria and I would sit together in the stands, usually by ourselves so we could focus on P.K. and keep our conversations about what was going on private. People knew what was happening. It's easy to see when one player is getting negative feedback.

The team manager's job included dealing with the complaints of twelve to fifteen sets of parents. Maria and I scheduled a meeting with him to discuss our concerns around messaging. Hockey parents worry, especially when we feel our children are not being treated fairly. This is not uncommon in a school or hockey environment. The world will not always speak to our children and treat our children the way we would want it to.

Our beef was about what we felt was happening to P.K.'s self-esteem. Children are resilient, but their self-esteem sits on their achievements, and the acceptance, feedback and support they receive from the significant adults in their lives. When their achievements and contributions are not recognized, when they no longer feel good about their environment and the joy is missing, that is when they lose motivation and inspiration.

The team manager listened to us, and he assured us he would communicate our grievances to the coach. I don't remember a follow-up conversation or meeting with the team. The next step was to wait and see if P.K. would feel better and if our anxiety would be alleviated. It wasn't, so we removed him from the team.

In the aftermath of my decision to pull P.K. from the Red Wings, what mattered most to us was figuring out how to get our son playing competitive hockey again. My actions were meant to remove P.K. from what Maria and I felt was a harmful situation so he could continue to develop into an excellent hockey player. What I wasn't looking for was to become the talk of the Greater Toronto Hockey League—but that, to my dismay, is exactly what happened.

Everybody knows that parents are capable of bad behaviour. I have witnessed parents wrestling, yelling and screaming. I have yelled and even broken a hockey stick when my emotions slipped away. I have been blinded by emotion, and when this happens, it makes it difficult to see why you are there in the arena. I was now the "problem parent."

People love to talk, and I gave GTHL parents something to talk about. People I met wanted to know what drove me to do what I did. My response was always this: "I could tell you my side of the story, but P.K.'s team is not present to give its side of the story. It would not be fair to them and my family." This killed the conversation immediately, at least while I was in earshot.

The main question people were asking was, "When will P.K. play again?" The rumours were that P.K. would not get his release from the Red Wings. In the GTHL, you sign with a team and register with the GTHL and Hockey Canada. That team owns your rights until the end of the season. The Red Wings were under no obligation to release P.K., and there was still a lot of season left. We pulled P.K. from the team in October, and the season runs until March or April. I know no one gets released overnight, but days were turning into weeks.

For our family, it was if time had stopped. The last thing I'd wanted to do was to get in the way of P.K. progressing up the hockey ladder. I began to have second thoughts about the decision I'd made in the heat of a moment. For what seemed to us like an eternity, P.K. had no team to call his own.

All these years later, Maria still believes I did the right thing, but I wish that I had at least followed the twenty-four-hour rule. Hockey is an emotional game. The unwritten rule is to wait twenty-four hours after a game if you have something to say to the coach, or if a coach has something to say to you.

I also could have used the advice I so often gave students who had difficulty controlling their emotions. I used to draw a stick figure riding a horse. "The galloping horse is anger," I would say. "That is you riding the horse. You are controlling it. As the horse gallops faster and faster, it represents anger growing. And if you don't do the right thing, you will fall off the horse and hurt yourself and others. You have to pull on the reins to control the horse. Slow the horse down, get off and walk away from the anger and take some deep breaths." I'd wait a moment for the image to sink in and then I'd ask the student, "Who is in charge?"

"I am, Mr. Subban."

"You are right," I would reply.

But on that game day when I pulled P.K. off his team, my emotions got the worst of me and I let go of the reins.

P.K.

When you are ten years old, all you think about is playing the game. I don't care where you are playing or what sport you are playing. Any kid playing a sport at nine or ten years old should just be able to do that—play the sport and have fun and enjoy the game and enjoy working with your peers and learning how to be a good teammate.

There were times during my minor hockey career when it wasn't about me getting more ice time—it was about me being able to play a sport I love while having fun and getting better at it. But it was also about my parents being able to protect me from being emotionally damaged. I think in a lot of cases, certain things happened and they were addressed in a way my parents thought was the right way at that time. My parents aren't perfect, but I'm sure they look back and wouldn't change anything they've done because, obviously, a lot of things they've done have worked out.

At the end of day, I think the majority of parents in hockey see their kids through rose-coloured glasses. My parents aren't like that. They have always been able to address me in a way where if I make a mistake, they say, "P.K., you can't do this or do that." But when it was time for them to stand up for me, they made the decision to take me out of an environment that was toxic, and away from what they thought could be a detriment to me being a good hockey player and continuing to just have fun.

I don't regret anything my parents have ever done, or that I have done. You live and you learn, and I think there are positives and negatives to everything. People may look at that and say, "Could he have waited till the end of the game?" Maybe he could have, but he made a statement doing that. He stood up for me and I will stand behind him.

As I recall, there was an agonizing wait before we heard from P.K.'s team. The Red Wings called and invited us to a meeting with team president Rick Cornacchia and Harry Evans.

I was filled with nervous tension as I drove into the parking lot and walked into the arena. P.K., Maria and I were joined by my good friend, David Bince. David knew hockey, and he was also a principal. I wanted him to speak on our behalf so my emotions could stay out of the discussion. He was a trusted friend who would not hesitate to tell me if I was wrong in the way I was dealing with the team. I knew enough not to go into that meeting with smoke coming out of my ears. What was done was done. I had my tail between my legs and wanted to do what was right for P.K.

My son waited outside the room, but David came in with us. I introduced David to Rick Cornacchia, and I remember exactly what Rick said: "This is a matter between the hockey club and the family. Karl, if you insist on having your friend being a part of this meeting, it's over." It was an easy decision for us to make but a difficult one for my friend, who had wanted to help.

The meeting started without Dave, and with Rick saying he had never seen anything like this before. Everywhere he went people were asking him why P.K. was not playing hockey. He had received numerous phone calls about the situation. Rick made it clear that my actions had the power to affect P.K.'s future in hockey. I said I did not want to be the reason P.K.'s hockey dream would end up on the shelf. This was the time to swallow my pride and say the right things and do the right things. This wasn't just about hockey, but about life too.

The meeting ended with no guarantee P.K. would get his release to play with another team in the GTHL that season. Rick had suggested P.K. play for the Ontario Minor Hockey Association, but the regular travel outside Toronto would have been too much for our family. We went home with our fingers crossed. The meeting gave us some hope, but the rumours we heard were that P.K.'s season, at least in Toronto, was finished. There was one other option Maria and I had started to discuss: my parents were living in Sudbury, and we were considering having P.K. go to live with them so he could play minor hockey in my hometown.

Maria and I played the situation over and over in our minds and hoped for a quick resolution. We missed being part of a team. We missed the drive to the rink and drinking coffee and tea to keep us warm in the cold arenas. We missed the feeling of seeing our kid on the ice doing what he loved to do. We missed the conversations with the parents. When and where would P.K.'s skates next touch the ice for a team in a meaningful game or practice? We had no idea, but we prayed. I believe that God always answers our prayers. The thing is, He never tells when He will answer them.

Soon after our meeting with the Red Wings, the phone rang. It was good news: P.K. had been released by the Red Wings and would play for the Mississauga Reps, another AAA team in the GTHL. One of the parents on the Reps had bought into the Red Wings and a player transfer was arranged. I don't know who initiated it, but this was the news we'd been hoping for, and wrapped in it was the second chance I wanted for P.K. Without a second chance in life, many children would have no chance at all. We did not take it lightly. P.K. could play hockey again. He was free to leave the penalty box I had created for him and not only pursue his hockey dream but also have fun, like all ten-year-olds should.

The Mississauga Reps were a middle-of-the-pack team, while the Red Wings were an elite team, but it didn't matter to us; we never saw the move as a demotion. We saw it as a good move because the team wanted P.K. At the time, P.K. already had a reputation as a good player, big and strong with a very hard shot—and other kids also wanted to play with him.

For all that P.K. had to offer the Reps, the new team was a great place for him to land. The coach, Martin Ross, had wanted to sign P.K. months before, but we had already committed to the Red Wings. The Reps' looser environment suited P.K.'s abilities and playing style. And the reality of the situation was that the Red Wings didn't need P.K. to win games. The Reps, however, did.

His first game with his new team was like something out of a Disney movie. It was a Friday night and the Reps would be playing, of all teams, the Red Wings, on the Red Wings' home ice. In the weeks leading up to the game, we had heard rumours that we had played the race card to find him a new team; that we blamed P.K.'s troubles on the fact he was he was black. I never saw it that way, or thought that way. Now, here we were and the talk was that the Red Wings were going to "take out" P.K. The crowd had come to see a spectacle, to see the powerhouse Red Wings destroy P.K. and the Reps.

At the time, I was in the habit of video-recording all of P.K.'s games. That night, I started to press the record button and then stopped. The tension in the atmosphere was too much to bear. The view through the camera lens was so narrow. I couldn't see everything that was going on, and on this day, I knew I wanted to see everything and feel everything and hear everything. The bleachers were packed and there was electricity in the air. I had never seen anything like it for a minor hockey game that was not a championship game. The referee dropped the puck and the game was on. What a feeling! This was the feeling I had missed, watching my son play in a GTHL hockey game. It turned out to be perhaps the most impressive game of P.K.'s minor hockey career. P.K. scored four goals and assisted on a fifth. One goal was particularly memorable, when he skated down the wing and shot the puck over the goalie's shoulder into the top corner of the net. When the final horn sounded, the Reps had upset the Red Wings at home, 5–1. Martin Ross says people still talk about P.K.'s performance that night. "It was the best game P.K. ever played," Martin says.

The adults came in droves that night to watch kids play a kids' game, and those young players did not let us down. They played, entertained and had fun. The win, ultimately, was not important. I was reminded that night why our children play the game and why we take them to the rink.

Looking back, however, that is the one game I wish I had on videotape.

The next day, we did it all over again. The Reps hosted the Red Wings at the Beatrice Ice Gardens. I think we lost the game 5–2. We took the first game and the Red Wings took the second—our hockey world was back to normal; the stars were lined up again.

P.K.

I remember that first game back. I've always been the type of player who enjoys those moments, when everybody is watching. You've got to step up and make a difference, and it was a game that was obviously very emotional for me. Ultimately, I was excited to play against my old teammates and wanting to beat them.

I played for a coach, Martin Ross, who enjoyed that moment and had a lot of fun with it. We are still very close friends today. He works within my company handling my memorabilia and merchandise. Martin is a character, and I remember laughing a lot and being loose before that game. That is probably why I was able to go out and play that well.

For me, hockey is not complicated. I enjoy the game and I just go out there and have fun. At the end of the day, it wasn't about whether I was going to play hockey again. I knew I was going to play.

I played for a lot of [struggling] teams like the Reps in minor hockey. It's not so much that you get used to losing, it's that you get used to your teammates relying on you. I have always been one of those players where the guys around me can rely on me to step up and make plays when the game is on the line. To me, that is how you define yourself as an all-star or superstar, as one of the best players in the game.

Ultimately, the situation worked out for the best for P.K. And I realized something crucial about minor hockey: what matters most is not winning games but facing challenges. Facing adversity is just as important as learning to skate, shoot and stickhandle. A young player must learn to deal with the challenges that come with playing, such as working hard to win on a team like the Reps. If winning comes too easy, you don't get as much of a chance to grow and develop.

At that age, what is more important than winning is developing good habits and a strong character. On the drive to that first game for the Reps against P.K.'s old team, I told him, "P.K., you have to go out there and show them the type of hockey player you are." We got him back out on the ice while he still had his confidence. He went into that game as a ten-year-old and did what he did. That took more than hockey skills. His inner toughness was starting to take shape.

If P.K. had stayed with the Red Wings, I'm not sure how much better he would have become. But I know that, as a team, the Reps had to work harder than their opponents, and they had to work together to have success. In the end, that was good for P.K. Coach Martin Ross was a huge part of the positive experience. I liked his approach. It was more in line with coaching children than what we'd experienced with the Red Wings. In minor hockey, too many coaches treat the kids like they are NHLers—and they are not.

P.K.'s dream of playing in the NHL was still alive, and he was learning valuable lessons with the Mississauga Reps. That team didn't hit the ice and know they were going to earn two points for a win. They weren't sure if they would get one point for a tie. Most of the time, they got zero points, but they were learning what they had to do to get two points.

While writing this book, I called Harry Evans. I am so grateful he agreed to be interviewed. This is what he remembers about P.K.'s short time with the Red Wings:

HARRY

P.K. had played for the Junior Canadiens in novice-level hockey with Steven Stamkos [during the 1998–99 hockey season]. They won the city championship that year and the Carnation Cup. The following year, each coach goes out and they try to recruit players. I had a meeting with Karl and talked to him about the opportunity for P.K. to come play for the Toronto Red Wings' minor atom team. We had a pretty good team. We were in the top three at that time. After meeting on several occasions and at the rink, they decided to come with us to the Red Wings. The tryouts were in April that year. So we picked the team in April and we played summer hockey. P.K. played with us, probably about fifteen or twenty games in the summer.

Then we shut down for July, and August camp came. It went well, and then we started the season with the early bird tournament, which we won. We started playing our regular season right after Labour Day weekend. I guess it was probably mid- to late October, we were about fifteen to sixteen games into the regular season, and Karl one night—I forget who we were playing against, but he told P.K. it was time to leave during the game. P.K. left the bench and went off the ice. I was in the middle of the game so I never said too much. I went into the change room after the game and P.K. wasn't there; he had left. The next day I phoned to see what the issue was.

Karl said, "This is not going to work out and we'd like to have a release for P.K."

I said, "At this time, I can't, because we only have the legal amount of players to play." Which was fifteen. I had to get a player to replace him before I could let anyone go.

Rick Cornacchia was the president of the Red Wings at that time, so I called him up and told him the story and he asked, "Well, what are you going to do and do you have anybody?"

I didn't, and I started making some calls.

At that time, the Red Wings had been sold to new owners, Paul Fenwick and Randy Hebscher. Paul's boy, Zack Fenwick, happened to be in the same age group as P.K. He was playing for the Mississauga

Reps. So we eventually talked and Fenwick came to the Red Wings and P.K. went over to the Reps. It took about a week to make sure Zack was okay with coming to the Red Wings.

Then we had a meeting with Karl, myself and Rick. The meeting was probably twenty to twenty-five minutes long. Karl said he wanted P.K. to leave; that it wasn't a good fit. He didn't think that it was going to work out and asked for his release.

[After Karl left the room] Rick asked me my opinion. I said, "I'd like to keep him but at the same time it is no good if they're not happy and it's not going to work out."

Rick asked, "Are you legal with the players?"

I said, "Yeah, young Fenwick wants to come here. We'll be legal."

And at the point we gave him an outright release. [P.K. played for the Reps two weeks after he left the Red Wings.]

I think most coaches have a twenty-four-hour rule or a forty-eight-hour rule. I think it gives everyone a chance to calm down, cool off, get their thoughts collected, have an opportunity to talk to the boy at home in private, find out really what was the story. At a lot of arenas, you're at one side of the arena and the parents are way over at the other side. They only see from their perspective. They don't know what happened at the game. They don't know if a kid came off a play and he was hurt, so that's why he missed a shift, for instance. And the game is heated. The game is played with emotion and a lot of times it gets too emotional and things get said at that particular minute that people regret.

On that particular night, yes, I feel Karl acted inappropriately. I remember Karl came up behind the bench and said, "P.K., it's time to leave." P.K. looked at me and I said, "Well, you've got to do what your dad says." Karl never got mad at us. Nothing was said. Nothing derogatory. No yelling or screaming. He just told P.K. it was time to leave and that was it.

Harry was asked if he was aware of our concerns about P.K.'s self-esteem being harmed by the way P.K. was being coached, and that he was being treated differently than the other players.

HARRY

They never said that to me. That's the first I've heard of it. At the time, there were only two centres and P.K. was one. You're trying to get everyone in the game, and in the particular game when P.K. left, we started off real slow and ended up taking three penalties in a row, so we were playing five-on-three. For the first six to seven minutes of the game we were playing five-on-three and we had a deep team. We were coaching in a minefield, trying to keep everybody happy. You're trying to get everybody in. We were trying to get at least four or five guys into the game early and we killed the penalty off but were still trying to get all the wingers into the game in the five-on-three situation over six or seven minutes of the game. [No one sat for ten minutes.] I guess that was the turning point, and they didn't like it that P.K. never went on the ice every second shift. Because he was one of two centres, in normal, regular shifts he's on the ice every second shift.

In regards to treating him any differently, I tried to treat him like everybody else. If he felt that, I hope it never hurt his desire to play or his willingness to play, or the family's willingness to be in the game, but I don't feel that I tried to treat him any differently. I tried to include him.

There was no prior mention of, "You know, Harry, can we have a talk?" There was none of that. And if there had been, that would be the thing that I would have liked to have done. If I could have handled it differently, it would be to say, "Let's sit down and see if we can talk this out." But sometimes you look back at it and you didn't get that opportunity. And the easier way to deal with it was to let it happen the way it did. That's the only regret I have, that I would have loved to finish out that year with him and then if he parted company, oh well, that's the nature of GTHL hockey. That's why there are twelve teams and you can move around.

I always stayed in touch with P.K. There were never any issues. In Malcolm's midget year, Malcolm played with the Reps (I was coaching a Reps team at a different level), and I used to always see P.K. and Karl and Maria around. We always said hello. I've always enjoyed the family. Karl was always running around with the other boys but Maria was so dedicated to P.K. She was the one who basically followed P.K. to every rink, every game. Maria is a very, very nice person. Very down to earth. Karl was more the guy who would stand up and talk to you. He's the school principal. He's not afraid to talk. But we've always been cordial with each other and I've never harboured any hard feelings.

I enjoyed the time P.K. was with us. P.K. was a fun kid and he's all about having fun. I wish it had worked out. I liked the kid and he had good skill set. When he was young he had a good work ethic. There aren't a whole lot of kids I know, who at six-thirty or seven in the morning would be at Westwood Arena by themselves to get a half hour or hour working on their game. It was just P.K. and a bunch of pucks on the ice. I walked in and I caught him there many times over the years. Just by himself, working hard. At an early age you could see the drive in P.K. And he had the support of his parents.

What happened with the Toronto Red Wings was quickly water under the bridge. Years later, when P.K. was playing in the OHL for the Belleville Bulls, I met Harry at a game in Barrie, Ontario, between the Bulls and the Barrie Colts. Harry lived close by and had come to see one of his former players—P.K. Subban. Harry was happy to see us and very proud of P.K. and his accomplishments. He did not shy away from us; instead, he came to sit with us.

Harry is still a respected coach in the GTHL, now with the AAA Mississauga Reps, coaching boys thirteen to fifteen years old. Every year, he and many thousands of others across Canada do something to make children happy—volunteer their time and energy so boys and girls can play hockey. Without them there is no game. And if Harry is reading this, I would like to say, "I like your game, Harry. Thank you for all you do for children."

9

Malcolm in the Middle

Saturdays and Sundays were hockey mornings in the Team Subban household, from wall to wall. The main floor hallway was the arena for fierce mini-sticks games. Like an old boxing ring, that floor was the scene of many battles, and it was streaked with tears, sweat and even a drop or two of blood. The hockey photos covering one wall created the perfect backdrop for our in-house arena. The other walls had dents and black stick marks that served as evidence of fun and competition, goals and celebrations—evidence that has long been washed away. The walls have been repaired and painted, and Taz and her husband and three boys have moved in and made it their home, but the echoes of those contests live on.

Jordan was the most dedicated of the hallway rink rats. On weekends, Maria and I would try to sleep in just a bit longer, but by 7 a.m., Jordan would be in the hallway. He'd empty a laundry basket, anchor it with shoes and set it up as his net. The hockey pucks were rolls of tape, tennis balls, a rolled-up sock—whatever his creative mind settled upon. Jordan would deke imaginary players, score on imaginary goalies and win every one of his imaginary games. We would tolerate his playing—until he decided to become his own referee. Jordan would get his hands on a whistle—an item that wasn't hard to find in the home of a principal and coach—and that would be it for any hope of a weekend lie-in for Subbans young and older. The yelling to "BE QUIET!" would soon start, but Jordan tuned us all out like so many heckling fans in the stands.

Jordan did not always play alone. On many weekend mornings, Maria and I would wake to the sounds of sticks on sticks, bodies on bodies, bodies hitting walls, a laundry basket hitting the front door and loud screams of "Goal, goal, goal!" or "You're cheating!" In that hallway shinny game, P.K. and Jordan would compete against each other to see who could score the most goals on Malcolm in net. P.K. would laugh the loudest, scream the loudest and shoot the hardest on Malcolm, who would be on his knees playing the game of his life. Sometimes Malcolm and Jordan would complain to us about P.K.'s sportsmanship, but we knew enough not to get involved. The game would eventually end when Malcolm and Jordan had had enough of P.K.'s tactics.

Malcolm in house league

Whether it was on the backyard rink, the shinny rink, or in the hallway with his brothers, Malcolm always made a beeline for the middle of the net. When he started out in house league, he jumped at every opportunity to play net. He even chose to be goalie the time I coached a soccer team.

And yet, I did not see goaltending in Malcolm's future. He was always one of the fastest skaters on the team; he was also a deft stickhandler and a sniper as a goal scorer. When I coached him, and when he was pushed, he would skate through the whole team to score a goal if that was what we needed. I could always match him up against the other team's best players. I knew one day he would play at a very high level. Malcolm made the game look easy, so of course I wanted him to play out instead of playing in net.

Another factor was that we did not want to take on the added financial burden that comes along with playing that position if it was going to be just a passing fancy. Children sometimes suffer from toy-store syndrome—they don't want to pick just one toy, they want to take all of them. I believed Malcolm would grow to love being a player. The toy you buy and take home becomes the one you play with the most.

Malcolm was born in December, so he was always among the youngest players on any team. Despite his age, he was an advanced player, but socially he was painfully shy. When I brought him to his first hockey games, he wouldn't move off the bench to play. When the kids change lines, five players go on the ice and the next players move down, but Malcolm would stay put, and I'd see him staring up at me in the stands. I figured if I were coaching him we'd get rid of that problem, and I was right—so that's how I became his coach during his first six years of hockey, apart from house league. When Malcolm was six, I coached him on the Etobicoke All Star team, which was the entry point for select-level players. The deal I made with him was that in house league I was not his coach, so he got to be goalie, but when he played on Daddy's select team, he had to play out.

He used to drive me crazy during the warm-up for the All Star games. Guess where Malcolm would go? He'd be in the net. Then we moved on to A league, and eventually to AAA with the North York Rangers. Again, he'd drive me crazy in practice, always gravitating toward being in net. And I would give him "that look," the one that said, "Malcolm, *what* are you doing?"

Malcolm's interest in being goalie didn't wane as the years passed, so why not let him play in net, right? You have to understand how good a player he was becoming. I remember some of the top players in his age group—some of whom, like Ryan Strome, are in the NHL now—and Malcolm was right there with them every step of the way. Also, when I coached, we never had enough players, and Malcolm was one of the best in the age group. He made our team very competitive. In my judgment, in those early years, Malcolm was usually either the best player on his team or simply the best player in the arena. Malcolm knew he was good and played that way—when he wanted to.

One game from my time coaching Malcolm stands out. He was on a team of eight-year-olds, called the Super 8s, playing a team of nine-year-olds. We were losing 4–0 and Malcolm scored a goal at the end of the second period to make it 4–1. We got a goal from another player to start the third period to make it 4–2. But the older team scored again to go ahead 5–2. Then Malcolm turned on the jets. He scored a pure hat trick in that third period to tie the game 5–5. His talent was on full display for all to see. It was beautiful.

But Malcolm wasn't finished yet. The game went into overtime and Malcolm scored the winning goal. He scored five goals that game against older players. How could I stick a player like Malcolm in net?

Despite being our best player, sometimes Malcolm's play would leave me frustrated and asking myself, "Why doesn't he do more?" I brought in guest coach Kam Brothers to work with the team on individual skills development and team play—we needed a lot of work in both areas. But Kam's biggest frustration was with Malcolm's lack of passion and drive. Like me, he saw Malcolm's unlimited potential as a player, but he made the astute observation that Malcolm didn't play like he wanted to play.

Kam was right—and I didn't know what to do.

My last year of coaching Malcolm was with the GTHL's North York Rangers; after that season, Malcolm would enter the peewee division. I felt it was time to cut the umbilical cord and let Malcolm work with another coach. As well, with all three boys playing, coaching was becoming too demanding for me; I couldn't be in three places at the same time.

The first year in peewee is very competitive in minor hockey, and a time when scouts start their conversations about future prospects. We had spoken with some people from the Junior Canadiens, a AAA team, and they said they'd love to have Malcolm. I was thrilled. He'd have a chance to continue playing defence at an elite level. Everything was coming together.

But I was about to learn an important lesson in parenting. The trick in working with our children is not only seeing their potential but also seeing what's in their heart. I saw Malcolm only from the outside and had not yet connected the dots that took me to his core. I knew what I wanted for Malcolm, but I did not know what Malcolm wanted for Malcolm.

That changed one day in 2006. Taz said she needed to speak to me; it was important. She was there on behalf of Malcolm, acting as his family agent, and she had an important message: Malcolm did not want to play hockey unless he could play goalie. It was in the net, or off the ice completely.

Maria says Malcolm had always wanted to be a goalie; we just ignored him. Correction: I ignored him. But in that moment, I realized that I would not—could not—ignore him any longer. We can only know what's ahead of our children when we discover what's inside them.

MARIA

Malcolm said to me, "I want to play goalie."

I repeated it to make sure. "You want to be a goalie?"

And he said, "If you don't let me play goal, I don't want to play."

So that was it. He was going to be a goalie.

I told Malcolm he might need to play house league.

He said, "I don't care."

That's when I knew he definitely wanted to be a goalie. A kid playing AAA and he's willing to go back to house league. I told him house league kids can't play.

He said, "I don't care, Mom. I am going to show you I can play goalie."

People said we were crazy. It was all over the GTHL. "You turned a good defenceman into a goalie? Oh my God, what are you doing?"

As Maria said, we gave him the lay of the land, telling him he might have to start in A, or AA or AAA. But we promised we would do whatever we could to support him.

MALCOLM

Growing up in house league, I always wanted to be a goalie. When one kid didn't want to take his turn, then I always went in net. I remember when I was six or seven, we were having a scrimmage, blue line to blue line. I was in my player gear, I was still a defenceman, and I put on the goalie gloves and grabbed the goalie stick and I was playing in net for the scrimmage. One kid took a shot and it hit me in the arm and I started crying. My dad said, "Good! Now get out of the net!"

That was pretty funny. But it didn't stop me. Every chance I had to play goalie, I played. Growing up, the whole time, I wanted to be a goalie. When my dad stopped coaching me I was supposed to join one of a few peewee teams and I remember telling my sister Taz I didn't want to play anymore unless I could be goalie. Then I told my parents.

To be honest, I wish I could play every position. It's not that I didn't like being a player; it's just that I really wanted to be a goalie. When I watched the Don Cherry tapes, I always loved watching the goalie parts. I used to rewind and watch them over and over, even when I was a player.

Goaltending is just my passion. I love making the big saves. I'm a pretty competitive guy and I feel it's the most important position. As a goaltender, you have more control over being able to lift your team. I feel if I do my part, the team has a better chance of winning. I'm a big part of the team winning.

Competitiveness runs in our family. Both my parents are competitive. We definitely get it from them. I can't stand losing, especially to my family and friends. I hate being bad at anything. Either I won't stop playing it until I'm good, or I just don't play. It's one or the other, and it's usually I won't stop playing till I'm good.

I'm glad Malcolm felt he could share his decision with his eldest sister. You want your kids to have someone to go to. That was important for the children at school as well. A student may not want to come to Mr. Subban, the principal. But maybe they can go to the vice-principal or find another teacher who they feel comfortable speaking to about a situation.

Malcolm was special and I knew that. So did other people. Don Norman, his sixth-grade teacher, told me once, "Malcolm's going to be such a great athlete. He's going to be good at whatever he chooses to do." Malcolm was a member of Mr. Norman's skipping team. They would perform nimble-footed tricks for the Jump Rope for Heart fundraiser every year. Malcolm's jump-rope moves showcased his abilities: he had the flexibility of a gymnast, quick hands at the end of his long arms, and soft feet at the end of his long legs. His raw athleticism made me believe he would make a smooth transition from player to goalie.

But that didn't stop me from desiring a little proof.

One of the dads on P.K.'s team, Scott Strang, was a goalie coach, and I told him about Malcolm's ambition. He said he would come over to the backyard rink and shoot pucks at Malcolm. Malcolm did not have goalie gloves, so I gave him a baseball glove and watched from the bay window in the kitchen. After about half an hour of working with Malcolm, Scott came in and said, "You know what, Karl? I'm shooting the puck at him and he's not flinching. I'm shooting them at his head a little bit and he's not afraid of the puck." Scott said he could see Malcolm's energy and his passion. So that was the turning point. We said okay, that's it.

Malcolm faced one major difficulty in starting his new career as a goalie: finding a team. The Junior Canadiens did not want Malcolm now; they didn't need a goalie. I wanted him to play in the AAA loop in the GTHL; if it did not work out in AAA, we would try double AA, then single A.

Many hockey people were skeptical. Goaltending is a highly technical position, and Malcolm had not received any formal training. You can read a book about driving a car but it does not make you ready to take to the highway. By the age of twelve, a AAA goalie in Ontario would normally have had hundreds of hours of training. Malcolm was far behind in that department.

But I was still optimistic. Complementing his athleticism, Malcolm had confidence in his ability to defend his net. He wanted you to shoot at him because each shot carried a built-in challenge: "I dare you to score." After many conversations, some disappointments and many prayers on our part, Jamie Fawcett, coach of the GTHL's Toronto Young Nationals, signed Malcolm as his team's second goalie. Fawcett was a shrewd guy—he had Malcolm sign a goalie card and a player card. I suspected Jamie signed Malcolm because he felt he might give up playing in net and could be a big help to his defensive unit. It is easier to find a backup goalie in a pinch than it is to find an elite AAA defender.

Malcolm's first game in goal was at Westwood Arena in north Etobicoke. I had butterflies in my stomach; it was unbelievable. Maria and I could not make ourselves walk into the arena to watch him play. The complex has five ice pads and Malcolm was on Rink 2. The doors have small square glass windows, and that is how we watched the game, nervously shuffling and peeking through the fog.

MARIA

His first game I said, "They are going to pepper him with shots and they are all going to go in, one after the other."

But Malcolm stood on his head and those goals were not going to go in.

HE WON THE GAME! Oh Lord, I tell you. He won the game.

Memory can be a funny thing. Maria and I remember Malcolm winning his first game, but Malcolm has a different recollection.

MALCOLM

We tied 1–1. We played a team called Regional Express Yellow. The one thing I remember is there was a scrum behind the net, or in front of the net, and I was just watching the scrum and the puck came out in front of the net and I wasn't paying attention to the puck. They didn't score, but I realized I'd better watch the puck.

By the time I started my second game, my nerves went away and I was thinking, "Oh, this is easy." I had tied my first game. The second game I got lit up for six goals and we lost 6–5. That brought me back down to earth.

I did well that first year and can't remember if I was named best goalie, but what I think helped was how hard coach Jamie Fawcett was on me.

Eventually, Maria and I were able to triumph over our nerves and watch the games from the stands, as we always had done as supportive parents. I know now that it wasn't my nerves that were the problem as Malcolm learned to play goal; it was my fear he would fail. But Malcolm wasn't afraid. One of his early games was against the talented Toronto Marlboros, again at Westwood Arena. They were the winningest team in our division. Our team was outplayed and outshot, but Malcolm made save after save. I think that game ended in a tie.

Malcolm's play throughout the season turned the doubters into believers. His passion and raw ability stood out, despite his lack of training in the position. Malcolm had arrived as a goalie, giving Maria the opportunity to sing the goalie song, "Holy Moly, What a Goalie," following every save.

The next season, Malcolm played for the Toronto Marlboros (a.k.a. the minor midget Marlies), sharing the goalie position,

Karl, Patrick and Markel in front of
our first apartment on Peter Street in
Sudbury; Mom is watching us from
the porch

Mom in Sudbury

The family: Patrick, Markel, Dad, Mom, Karl, Hopeton

Maria and her sister Claudine

Playing for Lakehead University

My dad and mom with Maria and me on our wedding day

Teaching at Cordella Avenue Public School in Toronto

Karl and Betsy, the Toyota Corolla that was also a member of the family

P.K. at the Brampton outdoor skating rink

P.K.'s first year playing hockey

Steven Stamkos, P.K. (age 9) and Justin Troiani with the North York Junior Canadiens

Malcolm the goalie

Jordan in house league

Tasha, P.K. and Taz by the organ that the girls played

At the 2007 NHL draft, 43rd overall pick P.K. Subban with Montreal Canadiens General Manager Bob Gainey (credit: Dave Sandford, Getty Images)

Karl and Élise Béliveau, in the P.K. Subban Atrium of the Montreal Children's Hospital

Karl and Maria with P.K. on the day he received the Meritorious Service Medal from the Governor General of Canada in Montreal

Karl at the Sochi Olympics

Nastassia's wedding

Our grandsons Epic and Honor enjoying cocoa at the rink, a family tradition

Maria with our granddaughter, Angelina

and they ended up winning a number of high-profile tournaments, including the city championships. Malcolm was pulled a number of times due to poor play, but he did not lose confidence. He possessed the physical tools and now, through game experiences, he was growing mentally.

When Malcolm was sixteen years old, he was drafted by the Belleville Bulls of the Ontario Hockey League. Draft day in May 2009 started with optimism. However, the wait time before your name appears (the OHL draft is done via computer) can be a confidence killer. There are twenty teams in the OHL, and each has at least one pick per round. During the months, weeks and days leading up to the OHL draft, we were not given any indication of where Malcolm would go. On that day, his name did not come up till the eleventh round—the 218th player out of 300 chosen.

We were all disappointed with Malcolm's draft position, and he was almost in tears. But the draft did communicate clearly to Malcolm, and to us, the amount of work he had ahead of him. Disappointment is not a bad thing if you see it as an appointment with success. The way the scouts saw Malcolm did not match the way he saw himself and his potential.

Malcolm was thrilled to be drafted and to be going to Belleville. He would be continuing Team Subban's relationship with the Bulls, which had started with P.K. I have always remembered what David Branch, commissioner of the OHL and Canadian Hockey League (CHL), said to players and parents at the minor midget banquet: "Playing hockey in the OHL is an opportunity and not a privilege." Playing for the Bulls was

Malcolm's opportunity to further his dream and move up the hockey pyramid.

Malcolm went to the Bulls' rookie camp in the spring and main camp at the end of August. Although he performed well at both, he did not make the team and was sent back to Toronto to work hard and develop his skills.

In his heart, Malcolm believed he was ready to play for the Bulls, but it was not his decision to make. The team's coaching staff knew best, and I felt they had made a decision that was best for Malcolm. Adversity is beneficial for our children. Like a spoonful of Buckley's, adversity may not taste good, but it's good for you. Malcolm had to ask himself, and not for the last time, "Will I allow this setback to make me or break me?"

There was another setback waiting for Malcolm in the hockey weeds, ready to pounce. What we didn't know coming back to Toronto was that the team he had played with the year before had signed a second goalie. Now they had two goalies, and Malcolm was no longer a Toronto Marlboro. He was Malcolm in the middle of nothing. That was a low point for him—a very low point. The only team he had was Team Subban.

Malcolm was frustrated, and we all felt helpless. But if there was one thing we knew, it was that waiting teaches patience and teaches you not to take your opportunities for granted. We had waited before and knew something would happen. And sure enough, by the end of September Malcolm found a team: the Mississauga Reps came calling.

That season, Malcolm worked hard, and he and his goalie partner defended the team's net all the way to the finals of the

TELUS Cup—the Canadian AAA Midget Championships—in Lévis, Quebec, in April 2010. As the tournament went on, Malcolm played better and better, earning the right to play in net in the final game, which was televised nationally on TSN. He stopped fifty-five shots, but the Reps, playing in their first national final, were edged 3–2 by the defending champions, the Notre Dame Hounds of Wilcox, Saskatchewan. Malcolm was the story of the final, and his performance solidified his reputation as an excellent goalie prospect.

Looking back, I have no regrets about how we handled Malcolm. I wanted all the boys to be good skaters. Normally, goalies don't do a lot of power skating, and even when they do have it, they are not doing the drills. One of Malcolm's biggest assets today in net is his ability to skate and handle the puck. Being a player also taught him a lot about shooters and shooting.

I'm glad we made it possible for him to follow his passion. It wasn't our dream for him to become a goalie, but because *he* wanted to do it, it was easy for him to sell us on the idea. One of the most important things you can do for your child is listen. Whenever they start making their own decisions, especially about the goals they want to pursue, you have to pay attention.

After a year playing in the OHL, Malcolm made the national junior team, and played at the World Junior Championships in Russia. When he was eighteen years old, Malcolm was selected in the first round of the NHL draft by the Boston Bruins. Dressed in his draft suit, tailored just for him, Malcolm walked to the stage in Pittsburgh, Pennsylvania, to meet his new bosses and to model his new jersey for the crowd and the cameras. Tears of joy were running down his face, like raindrops on a window. Malcolm was emotionally charged that day, and for good reason. He had trained hard and played hard for years, hoping for this day to come, for his name to be called.

For Malcolm—and for P.K. before him and Jordan after him—the NHL-calibre player the hockey world saw on draft day was forged in a small town on the eastern shores of Lake Ontario, playing with and against some of the best young players in the world, under the watchful eye of a demanding yet caring coach who knew how to develop young men, on and off the ice.

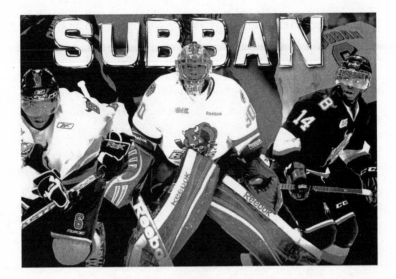

10

Bullish on Belleville

Getting our children started in minor hockey was as easy as one, two, three. You register them to a house league, dress them in their uniform and let them learn how to play the game. The transition into junior hockey, however, was not something we could count on.

There is no guarantee your child will be drafted and then make the team. Approximately five hundred thousand boys and girls register every year to play minor hockey across Canada. Only twelve hundred of them, ranging in age from sixteen to twenty, play on the sixty teams in the Canadian Hockey League,

North America's top amateur league. Making it to the CHL—
which comprises teams from the major junior hockey leagues
in nine Canadian provinces and four American states—is sort
of like playing a game of musical chairs. There are many more
players than opportunities to play in the premier junior league
in the world.

When the music stopped, each of my three sons found a
chair with the Belleville Bulls of the Ontario Hockey League.
When the Bulls drafted sixteen-year-old P.K. in 2005, little did
we know that the organization would draft all three of our
boys. It was the beginning of a relationship that lasted ten years
on the calendar but a lifetime in our hearts.

When P.K. was drafted, we knew that making the team was a
long shot. Although we were confident in his ability to play
hockey, and play at that level, the decision was not in our hands.
The OHL draft took place in May that year. We went to the OHL
website—no password required—and followed the draft live.
After an agonizing wait through the first five rounds, we finally
saw P.K.'s name appear in round six. Shortly after, George Burnett,
coach and general manager of the Bulls, called our home to speak
with P.K. He welcomed him to the Bulls organization, and with
that, P.K. felt a lot better about his hockey dream.

We did not do a lot of celebrating because the job was not
done. Some hockey families we knew had planned draft parties
with relatives and close friends. We did not feel comfortable
doing that. Because P.K. was drafted in the middle rounds, he
was not guaranteed a spot. Also, the Bulls had taken a number
of defenders ahead of him. Some time ago, a hockey parent
told me that with the OHL it is not the round you come in on
that matters, but the round you go out on. I have never

forgotten the message, and it helped me to guide P.K. through the draft process.

While some players in P.K.'s draft class had an advisor, we did not, so Maria and I had to use our common sense. Common sense told us to explore a second option for P.K., in case he didn't make the Bulls. We got in touch with the Milton Hawks of the Provincial Junior Hockey League. P.K. tried out with the Hawks and played an exhibition game for them. The coach liked him and was eager to have him on his roster. If the Bulls liked him more, however, it would be an easy decision for us to make, because the OHL is the best training ground in the world for future NHL players. So, off to Belleville we drove in Ruby Red, our Ford Aerostar van, to see how P.K. would do at his first OHL training camp.

P.K. trained hard that summer. Maria had a nephew, Clifford Dorsett, who lived in Cambridge, Ontario. Clifford told us about a trainer, Keith Vanderpool, who lived on his street. Maria made the connection and we were eager to join Keith's training group; P.K. would be around OHL players on the track and in the gym. An added bonus was the scrimmage Keith ran with pro and junior players. Over the course of that summer, we made the hour-long drive to Cambridge four or five times a week to train, sometimes twice a day. P.K. never complained about the grind. Maria and I were committed, so he was committed.

The training and skating pushed P.K. to another level, and he was willing to pay the price in order to be ready for the Bulls training camp. Our objective going in was simple—be the best player on the ice. P.K. was fast on the track but not the fastest. He was strong in the weight room but not the strongest. It was on the ice that he separated himself from everybody else.

The strategy paid off: training camp lasted forty-eight hours, and they were P.K.'s best forty-eight hours in hockey. Now it was up to the Bulls.

At the end of the camp, the coaching staff schedules private meetings with the players and their families. At that time, the player is given a verbal report card on his status with the team. Since *Subban* is close to the end of the alphabet, I figured it would be a while before we learned P.K.'s fate. But before we had a chance to move from our seats, an official approached us: team management wanted to meet with us right away because we were number one on their list. P.K. had changed out of his hockey gear and had his backpack on his shoulders when he met us in the hallway. We walked in as a family to meet coach and general manager George Burnett.

I had invited Keith Vanderpool to join Maria, P.K. and me for our initial meeting with the Bulls staff. P.K. was still wearing his backpack when we were shown our seats, as if he weren't planning to stay long. "Where do you think you're going?" George asked our son. P.K. just smiled. Then George asked, "Where did you learn to skate that way?" I don't remember P.K. answering, but I do remember that his smile got even bigger. Then George said something to P.K. that no one had said to him before. "P.K., I believe you will play hockey at least at the American Hockey League level." With that endorsement, I knew he would be a member of the Bulls.

We did not jump up and down, yell or scream in the Bulls office. We waited until we were in the privacy of our car. The car ride home from Belleville was never sweeter, shorter or faster.

———

Since we didn't have an advisor, I left matters in George's hands when it came time for P.K. to sign his OHL contract. If I was willing to trust him to coach and develop my son, I felt I could trust him with P.K.'s contract too. When the contract was ready, we all signed it, and P.K.'s status as a player in the OHL was official. His goal for training camp had been to be the best player on the ice. And now he would be playing with and against the best junior players in the world.

Our entire family was happy for P.K.'s accomplishment. Before he left home to begin his first season in the OHL, we had a backyard barbecue to celebrate with friends and family. Making the Bulls as a sixteen-year-old is reason to celebrate. It has been our family's tradition to celebrate birthdays with a big party, and as our children grew older, we added celebrations for academic and athletic achievements.

Maria's greatest worry during P.K.'s draft year was not if he would be drafted but where. She was far from thrilled at the idea of P.K. living and playing hockey in faraway places such as Sudbury or Sault Ste. Marie, or Erie, Pennsylvania, or Saginaw, Michigan. I was ambivalent. I did not want to rock the boat or make demands—getting in the way of my child's opportunity was not something that I subscribed to as a parent. However, I didn't blame Maria for wanting P.K. within arm's reach. And that was what Belleville offered, a mere two cups of coffee and two hundred kilometres along Highway 401. We have made so many trips to Belleville over the years that our car could drive itself there. The weather was not always great, but we made it ticket-free and accident-free for ten years.

———

As I have mentioned, my first car was a 1983 Toyota Corolla sports coupe, which was the previous year's model when I bought it new off the lot when I was still a student in Thunder Bay. We called it Betsy. I don't know where the name came from, or who christened it, or what it was supposed to mean, but Betsy served our family well. You could say it was lived in and broken in. Our five children grew up in that car, played in it, ate in it, got sick in it and slept in it. Mileage-wise, it probably went around the world a couple of times! I was very attached to that car, and as a result had it on and off the road for more than twenty-five years. During P.K.'s early years in Belleville, even though we had a van by then, I kept driving Betsy because twenty dollars in gas was all we needed for a round trip. With Taz in university and Malcolm and Jordan playing minor hockey, we had to do more with our dollar.

One time, we decided to take Betsy to Kingston, Ontario, about an hour east of Belleville. On the way home, as soon as I merged onto the westbound 401, I heard a noise coming from the back of the car. It was as insistent as a baby's crying— the kind of noise that makes you pay attention to it. I stopped when it was safe to do so and inspected my antique car. I am no mechanic, but I determined I should drive in the slow lane home with the hazard lights on. The brakes worked and the noise was minimal at low speed. So it was slow and steady in the right lane all the way to Toronto. When I took the car to a garage for inspection, I was told the wheel bearings needed some greasing. Betsy would live to see another day.

Another time, we were rushing to drive P.K. back to Belleville for his 2 p.m. weekday practice. As soon as we got into Cobourg, the rear driver-side tire peeled off the rim. The rubber began to hit the car, making a sound like a drummer in a marching band. P.K. didn't want to be late, and we didn't want him to be late—but the tire didn't care. Replacing the damaged tire with the doughnut would take time. I made the call I didn't want to make to the coach to let him know we'd be late. George had seen my Toyota, and I'm sure he was far from shocked to receive the news.

One day Betsy left us stranded at the side of the road in the area of Weston Road and Lawrence Avenue West in Toronto. Finally, we were compelled to buy a Chrysler K-Car. This no-frills economy car worked for us until it could not run anymore. And that is when we bought the Ford Aerostar, nicknamed Ruby Red. Despite buying other vehicles, we did not get rid of Betsy. On occasion, Betsy would be taken to the mechanic and be up and running on the road again.

After P.K. signed his NHL contract and was playing in Montreal, he bought me a shiny new black Ford Expedition. George saw that truck too, as it was now Malcolm and Jordan playing for the Bulls. I don't know what George's thoughts were when he saw me driving the new truck. One thing is for sure, though; he knows where we came from, and how far we had come.

I kept Betsy until the fall of 2013. I had just retired, and we were moving from our family home on Arborwood Drive in Rexdale to our new house in Nobleton, Ontario, and Maria unilaterally ruled: "You are not taking this piece of junk up to Nobleton." And so my beloved sidekick took her last trip: to the junkyard.

———

Malcolm and Jordan, along with Taz and Tasha, spent a lot of time in Belleville. They heard all the stories, both good and bad, about living away from home and playing hockey in an OHL city. These experiences removed the fear of the unknown, became the answers to our questions and grew into dreams for our boys to reach for. By the time Malcolm started in Belleville, he was more than ready.

MALCOLM

George Burnett was trying to instill professionalism in us as kids. We were sixteen to twenty years old and that's a huge part of a teenager's life. That can really define how you grow up as a person and can have a big influence on you later in life. He was preparing us for what we wanted to do and what we were trying to achieve—to be professional hockey players.

To be professional hockey players you have to act a certain way. You have to have good morals and be responsible. You have to take care of your body. He was trying to instill that in us and make it a safe environment. Some parents worry about their kids moving away at such a young age. He made it really comfortable and easy for us, and our parents as well.

The second time around, with Malcolm, was a lot easier than the first time with P.K. And by the time Jordan was drafted by the Bulls, we knew the script inside out.

The making of P.K., Malcolm and Jordan as professional hockey players started in Belleville with Coach George. There was media training through interactions with the press. There were magazine, newspaper, radio and television interviews, and we could see them getting better with practice. George was such a good role model that the boys would at times sound like him during radio and television interviews.

The boys dressed in their Sunday best on game days. We never saw them without their suits before or after games. After home games, players and families would meet at the same restaurant. The boys' behaviour was always exemplary. They all knew George had eyes and ears everywhere.

My boys owe a lot to George and his ability to develop potential. After P.K. played his first game in the NHL, he framed and signed his game-worn jersey and had it delivered to George as a sign of his gratitude.

George was trained to be a teacher, but he spent more years teaching with skates on and instructing from behind the bench than in front of a classroom. He is one of the best teachers I have ever met. I can only hope my grandkids will find a George Burnett along their hockey journey.

George played such an integral role in the development of our boys that I felt he deserved to have a say about his experience coaching Team Subban.

GEORGE

ON DRAFTING P.K. We are dealing with kids who are fifteen years old, and a lot of it is speculative, a lot of it is projections, and P.K. was a young man who played with great skill. Fewer players after the fourth or fifth round actually play, but I think a lot of that has to do with the commitment the player makes that first summer leading up to first training camp, and also the work they do in that first year, on and off the ice.

P.K. was very determined from the moment I first met him to be a part of our team, right from day one in training camp. He had every intention of putting the work in and coming to camp and earning the job.

It was special that we were able to find a player in the sixth round who turned out to be of his talent—the contributions he made and what he's done since. But it does happen, and we were fortunate he brought such a terrific attitude and work ethic and set of skills to the rink each and every day.

I first met Karl and P.K. at the Memorial Cup in London in 2005. We had just had our draft and the players came to the Memorial Cup for us to get a chance to meet them. I remember sitting in the courtyard of the John Labatt Centre and my impression of P.K. was of a very confident young man, but also very determined, and he made it clear to me he was going to do the work required.

I appreciate Karl—he's always been terrific, a real supporter of the program and our staff in general. I am not going to take credit for dealing with a young man who was very determined and a family that was extremely supportive through the ten years we worked closely with them.

COMPARING THE THREE BOYS: With each of the three boys, the circumstances were completely different. Our team was right on the verge of becoming a very good team in P.K.'s first year. His first year was a year we took a step forward as an organization. [I'd started in Belleville] the year before, and he was in the second group of draft picks that we made. It was a unique group and that was the start of, really, a four-year run where we were challenging to win championships. So with kids like P.K. taking on a big responsibility as young players in our program, it was kind of the backbone of four big years.

Malcolm was different. Karl directs a lot of credit to me. I think it's very important to say it's not coming on my shoulders for drafting Malcolm, P.K. and Jordan. I would say I was a little bit more involved in drafting Jordan, only because he wasn't a secret. It was a bit of a flyer to take Malcolm. He didn't even have a chance to go back to the team he played for the year before. When we did draft him, there wasn't a spot for him, so we put him to play with the Mississauga program and he went right to the finals. He had a big year of development and it has been a great example for us, for all the years we have been involved— whether it was P.K., who was a sixth-round pick, or Malcolm, who was an eleventh-round pick, here are two young guys who took advantage of an opportunity. They weren't wrapped up in being first-round picks or all the hype that goes along with it.

Malcolm came into camp the next year and we had him pencilled in to go to our affiliate team in Wellington. That was all set up, and with the family as well, kind of a great backup plan. We were strong in goal. We had drafted a young man in the first round the year before, the same age as Malcolm, Tyson Teichmann, who was the elite goalie in his age group. And we had the other top goaltender within our program at that time. We weren't looking for Malcolm to come and play, but he played so well in training camp we had no choice but to keep him.

It was a weaker team that year. We had a big graduation under the weaker group, so he played and ultimately had an opportunity to play on a young club. Two seasons later he's a first-round NHL draft pick.

I credit our goalie consultant at that time, Sebastien Farrese, who had a great relationship with Malcolm and worked very closely with him. But Malcolm was an athlete. He was tall and lean and looked like a track star. P.K. was a much heavier build and not nearly as tall. Malcolm was very quiet and didn't really have much to say at all—he just went about his business, got into a routine and took direction and took advantage of an opportunity. The rest was left up to him. He was a top player for our club in a championship-calibre year. We didn't win the championship but we went to Game 7. It was a conference final, in his final year, and a good situation for him as a nineteen-year-old.

Jordan is, again, another circumstance. He's playing on the best team in the province with the Marlies [the Marlboros]. He was highly rated. We were fortunate to get him at number five in the draft. There was talk of him going sooner.

Jordan was a different guy than the other two, but he came with all the expectations on his shoulders. The other two kind of came in under the radar and made their way. It was probably a tougher transition for Jordan.

The person I don't want to forget in this whole thing is Amy McMillan, who was the billet for all three boys. She played a big part in guiding these guys as well, opening her home to all three.

SETTING EXPECTATIONS: Our first meeting at camp we outline to the players and parents the expectations of the program. School is a priority, but when they are at the rink, we want that to be a priority. Being good people was always a part of our mandate, and making good choices. I think the kids will probably not admit it, but they like to have rules, they like to have structure. When they don't have that it's difficult, when they have to make all those decisions on their own. A lot of kids come into our program or come into our league with great expectations on them, but they are not willing to do the necessary things to take the next step.

In that first meeting, I would have used examples of kids who made our team the previous year, eighth-round picks or walk-ons. There is so much entitlement in the game, [but] the game doesn't owe you anything; you have to take advantage of the opportunities that are provided and make your own way. Those are the kids who surpass expectations and play the game. Perseverance is a big thing, and there is always going to be adversity along the way. You are going to have bad games; you are going to have bad nights; you are going to have injuries. There are all kinds of things that can pop up along your way, and how you deal with them is most important.

SUBBAN FAMILY VALUES: I think they are all grounded. It's not wrong for a kid to come in and have a car right from day one—lots do and that's okay. But I can still remember, I think P.K. was nineteen years old when he got his first vehicle and wow, that was special. That was a big deal. I think they always appreciated the things they had, as a family, and the time their parents spent and how much their parents cared for them. A lot of people forget there are two sisters in the mix here too who are very strong individuals as well. It's a unique family, and P.K. gets his fair share of the headlines, but it's a special group of people— and the grandkids are [going to be] in the draft in 2027 or whatever, so I hope I am around long enough to have to deal with it.

DEALING WITH RACISM: I think you have to recognize that for all three— but in P.K.'s case, being the first—for a young player, coming out of the city and now you are in rural Ontario, in a town of forty-five thousand people, that's a pretty significant social change. I know some of the things that P.K. had to listen to. I've seen social media. When Malcolm was in the World Junior tournament and they didn't win, I saw the nonsense and the garbage he had to deal with.

There were a number of times, particularly with P.K. and Malcolm, where they could have exploded or had a rebuttal or had a response, and they always took the high road. I think that is a reflection of Mum and Dad.

The city of Belleville is home to diehard hockey fans who love their Bulls. My boys have been on teams that won more games than they lost and on teams that lost more games than they won. But whatever happened on the ice, one constant was how they were treated by their fans. The fans cared. When the team won, the fans stood up and cheered. When the team lost, they did not lose hope or confidence. I sat in section 11 for ten years and never heard a negative comment directed at my family or my boys on the ice.

The fans made Belleville feel like a second home and our boys feel that they belonged to them. The fans made banners for all the players, including for my boys, especially in the playoff rounds. They would go above and beyond to make sure my boys were comfortable. They baked cookies and knitted clothing. One fan googled jerk chicken and curry chicken recipes and made them for my boys. The fans of Belleville were great cheerleaders for Team Subban. I hope we gave them as much as they gave to us.

Maria and I saw hundreds of Bulls games in Belleville. After each game, our boys' biggest fan would come over and chat.

Vivian is her name. She purchased and wore the boys' sweaters, starting with P.K., then Malcolm and Jordan. She is a symbol of the spirit and support we received from the fans in Belleville.

On Saturday, March 21, 2015, the Belleville Bulls played their final game of the season, losing 4–2 to the Barrie Colts. And it wasn't just a season-ender; it was also the final game for the Bulls in Belleville. The team had been sold and moved to Hamilton, Ontario, where it would become the Hamilton Bulldogs for the 2015–16 season.

There was not a dry eye in Yardmen Arena that night. It was a standing-room-only crowd. The trumpet player, who was always in our section, was blasting out his familiar hockey tunes. To my right I saw another regular, a super fan, crashing a pair of oversized cymbals. As the seconds disappeared off the giant scoreboard hanging over centre ice, all of the fans stood up, ringing cowbells. The noise was rattling our ears while the emotions melted our hearts.

This final game also marked the end of our formal relationship with the Bulls. Jordan went into the team's record book for scoring its very last goal and for being the scoring leader that final season, as the team faded into hockey history. At the final buzzer, the arena speakers lifted my spirits by playing the Irish Rovers' "Wasn't That a Party." It sure was: one we lived and one we loved.

11

Lessons from the Schoolyard

During many of those years when my weekends were spent in Belleville, my weekdays were focused on trying to make a difference in Toronto's Jane and Finch neighbourhood. When I moved to Brookview Middle School as principal in September 2006, I brought with me some of George Burnett's strategies as a parent, teacher and coach for getting the best out of young people. I was now the head coach, general manager and president of Brookview, a middle school of between four hundred and six hundred students in grades six, seven and eight. It was a school that had suffered too many losing seasons.

When I got my first look at Brookview, located in the heart of one of the city's most disadvantaged neighbourhoods, I have to say I wasn't left with the best first impression. It was late June, and I was at the school for a transitional meeting. While I was there, I did a walk-through to get a feel for the place.

Now, in all fairness, schools don't always look orderly that late in the academic year, when students are cleaning out their lockers and staff are changing rooms. It's to be expected that there will be some paper in the hallways, along with furniture, moving boxes and students wandering here and there. Be that as it may, when I saw two students sitting on the steps in the front foyer combing and braiding hair as if they were in a hair salon, it was an unwelcome sign. And I certainly did not appreciate seeing the graffiti on walls, lockers and doors.

I am sure there were positive things happening in the school, and I know and believe that first impressions, while important, are not everything. However, a school must look like a school and feel like a school. What children see becomes what they know. What they know becomes what they act out.

How the school looked and how the students looked were two things I started working on improving as soon as I took my post in September. It wasn't too long before the students heard my "looks and books" speech. The look was what I called the "Brookview look." You come to school wearing your school uniform and you follow the rules and routines. If you didn't have a uniform, we would give you one. If it needed to be washed, we would wash it. We started a uniform recycling program to help those families facing financial difficulties. I would also purchase uniforms and keep them in storage for students who experienced a middle-school growth spurt.

The look was also about behaviour. Brookview valued respect; it was about treating others the way you wanted to be treated. If I saw students in the neighbourhood, outside of school hours and off the property, I still wanted to see that same look. I told the students that their behaviour in the community was my business. If their behaviour was good, the school would look good and I would look good. I added that I had worked very hard for my good reputation, and asked them to please not ruin it.

The "books" part of my speech was about being prepared to learn, then working to learn. Looks and books are the two wheels on my bicycle. When you're on a bike, you only move forward when you pedal. Looks and books work the same way. They will only take you far in life when you do the right work.

Over time, I gave the school environment a total facelift. A "Welcome to Brookview" sign was painted in big blue letters just inside the main entrance; it became the first greeter for everyone who stepped through the front doors. A new bulletin board was installed in the front entrance to recognize the accomplishments of former students. The "Where Are They Now?" board featured Brookview graduates who were musicians, educators, writers, social workers, soldiers and athletes. I wanted children to know that the dream starts here—at 4505 Jane Street, Toronto. Who do you want to be and what do you want to do? You can tell them that they can achieve anything they set their minds to, but it is important for them to see it. The wall next to the "hair salon" steps now featured framed pictures of students working, playing and smiling. When green plants became new pieces of furniture in the front foyer, some staff did not believe the plants would last. That thought alone almost discouraged me, but I had faith the students would not harm those plants, and that faith was not misplaced.

Under my watchful eyes and ears, the students learned to be attentive to their steps, words and every move they made around me. To address the disorderly way they were moving in the halls between classes, we painted on the walls around the building "Walk to the Right." As time progressed, we were looking better, moving better and hopefully learning better too.

Punctuality was a major problem. I used to tell the children that Brookview Middle School was not a community centre—you couldn't just drop in whenever you wanted. Students would come rolling in at all hours, like waves on a Caribbean beach. When you arrive late every day, you will fall behind in your school work and your academics will suffer. It also lowers morale and hijacks learning. Walking in late is like ringing a doorbell. It steals attention. The teachers stop teaching and students stop learning.

One of the first strategies I used to deal with lateness was from George Burnett's playbook. One day, I received a phone call at work from George. That morning, P.K. had been in bed at his billet's house when he should have been in a chair in a classroom. The Bulls' assistant coach, Jake Grimes, monitored the players' school attendance daily and reported his findings to George, who did not mess around if his players were missing school. George called me, with P.K. also on the line from home. After that, I never had to worry about P.K. being late for school.

As Brookview's principal, I used my phone just like George did. My BlackBerry would be running hot each morning—if there were fifty late students, I made fifty phone calls. Many of the parents did not know their children were late until their phone rang.

I also developed a new strategy I called leading with a bell. During the playoffs, the Belleville Bulls would hand out cowbells to fans to make noise—and cowbells are loud. I brought one of those bells to school. The students would know when I was approaching—they would hear my cowbell before they saw me. When I was in the schoolyard in the morning, I would ring the bell to get students' attention or to signal that it was time to go inside.

Students learned that if they were late and they could hear my bell, they had better pick up the pace. There were some who would come in late and not report to the office; they'd try to sneak past me. Occasionally, to reinforce my message, I would send them home. My view was, "You have a right to an education, but you don't have a right to attend this school and operate according to your rules." By setting the tone in these ways, I saw improvements in punctuality—there were many mornings when my cowbell was ringing in an empty yard.

If I saw paper on the floor I picked it up. Soon, students were racing me to pick up the paper, pleased to find favour with their principal. On one occasion it was a teacher who raced me. He handed the litter to me, and told me with a smile that my campaign wouldn't make a difference. I took the paper and said, "Thank you." It wasn't for picking up the paper, but for his years of service. This teacher had done many good things over his years at the school, but this was not one of them. He transferred to a new school the following September.

You see, sometimes the action is more important than the motivation. If the students were picking up the trash just to please me, I was okay with that—because one day they would realize they were doing it for themselves too, and that it also happened to be the right thing to do. It is a lot better to do something in the moment to please me than to do nothing at all.

One day I asked the school caretaker for a bottle of cleaning agent and a rag. When I saw marks on lockers or walls, I cleaned them off. Just one mark left on a wall or a locker invited more marks. My "see it, clean it" philosophy worked beautifully. If students stopped to ask what I was doing, I would say, "I am cleaning the school for you. That's how much I care about you." Soon our school stopped looking like a graffiti exhibition.

As the principal I wanted to be a constant presence in the school. If the children were in the halls, especially when they were changing classes, I was there with them. When they were in the cafeteria eating lunch, I was there with them. When they arrived in the morning for school or were leaving at the end of the day, I was outside greeting them or saying goodbye. My eyes were always on them and my ears were attuned to their every word and sound. It was my job to know them and to help them to know me. You can't influence them if you are not spending time with them.

Brookview Middle School is located in northwest Toronto, not far from York University. One of the mottos of this institution of higher learning is "The Way Must Be Tried." Too few students from my school were finding the way to university. For many, destructive behaviour was getting in the way of making it there, or even graduating high school. York was so close to them but yet so far. Brookview was like an egg sitting in a nest of high unemployment and high crime rates, with a label and reputation that crushed hope and dreams.

Brookview Middle School had a United Nations look to it, which is reflective of the community. There were close to twenty different languages spoken, and English was not the first language for about 50 percent of the students. The neighbourhood is considered low income, with only approximately 15 percent of parents having a university education. Children from South Asian backgrounds were the most numerous, and those identified as African-Canadian were next in line. We had our share of English-as-a-second-language students and special needs students, although I didn't find we were over-represented in those areas.

Brookview's key feature was the number of students in regular classrooms who were struggling both academically and socially. The expectation among educators is that from kindergarten to grade two, students are learning how to read, and from grade three on, students are reading to learn. But among the sixth-grade students who started at Brookview, the majority were reading at only fourth-grade level. It's often said that education starts in the home, where the parents are the first teachers and the home the first classroom. When that home environment is disadvantaged, for any number of reasons, kids are way behind the starting line for school readiness. Like coaches, teachers need to make adjustments to their game plan.

One initiative I started was DEAR— Drop Everything and Read—and it became part of our afternoon routine. The first twenty minutes after lunch from Monday to Friday was silent reading time. Students became used to seeing me with a cowbell in one hand and a book in the other. If I wanted them to read I had to model the behaviour. Students were not allowed to walk around the school without their book. Anyone I found without a book would be served a notice to meet with the librarian.

This one activity took care of two needs. The transition between the lunch break and afternoon classes was always chaotic, like hosting a daily Black Friday stampede. The reading time served to calm the mad rush and help students focus for class.

During my career I worked in nine different schools as a teacher or administrator. Brookview was my most challenging assignment. I have told friends and family that I gave it my best effort, my own money and a couple spoonfuls of tears. I suffered from unrelenting stress, which I dealt with by not eating as well as I should and gaining weight. My family was concerned about my health—I became a diabetic during my time at the school. I had to think on the spot and act on the spot. I did not have the benefit of reflection because there would always be more fires to put out.

One such issue arose when students wouldn't throw out their waste from the fast-food restaurant next door, leaving the school floors littered with remnants of chicken wings and fries. Since DNA testing to pinpoint the culprits was not an option, I had to come up with a different solution. So one day, I picked up some of the pop cans and packaging and made myself a necklace, which became my fashion statement for two or three days. Everywhere I went, students wanted to know why I was wearing that necklace. I'd say, "I am wearing the necklace to protest those students who are refusing to use the trash bins and continue to dump their food garbage in my school." After about a week, the problem disappeared.

That same restaurant was also the source of another "fire." The establishment was well-frequented by the Brookview population, and too many students would wait to order their food until five minutes before the entry bell rang. So I had a chat with the owners of the restaurant and persuaded them not to serve our students in the fifteen minutes before the bell. Fire extinguished.

My first year at Brookview went mostly as I expected. I made time to get to know the students, staff, school programs and community. I was looking forward to the summer holidays and returning to work with the staff for the fresh start that comes with every new school year. But then something happened that turned our lives upside down.

On an ordinary school day in late May 2007, a ninth-grade student at nearby C.W. Jefferys Collegiate Institute, Jordan Manners, was shot in the chest in the school hallway. It was the first time a student had been shot and killed inside a Toronto school—a needless tragedy that left us all asking, *Why?* Two teens were arrested, and two trials followed, but it was never determined why Manners, who had just turned fifteen, was shot—whether it was an attempted robbery gone horribly wrong or an accident. There was no conviction in the case.

What hit those of us at Brookview especially hard was that Jordan had graduated the previous June from our school. I never met him—he was one of approximately two hundred eighth-grade students on that June day when I made my first visit. His death traumatized students, staff and the community, and placed our school in the spotlight again. We had made headlines in the

Toronto Star the previous year for having a record number of suspensions. Now, with one of our former students meeting such a tragic end, our school community was dealt a heavy blow.

It wasn't long after Jordan's death that a memorial display was created for him just outside the school's main office. Students and staff decorated a cabinet with photos and a T-shirt featuring his picture. A community member created a large, airbrushed portrait, and it, too, was on display, keeping his memory alive. Students walked around the school in slow motion and made the cabinet a meeting place. Jordan's funeral service was at the church next to our school, and when the church could not house all those who attended, I jumped at the chance to welcome them into our gymnasium, where we had hooked up an audio feed of the service. Students and staff helped to make our guests feel welcome and comfortable.

It was a sad ending to the school year, and I didn't think things could get any worse—but they did. Two months after Jordan's death and less than a month after graduating grade six at Brookview, eleven-year-old Ephraim Brown was attending his cousin's eighteenth birthday party on a warm summer night when he was shot and killed. Up past his bedtime, listening to music on his headphones, Ephraim was caught in the crossfire between two rival gangs. A bullet struck him in the throat, and he died on the sidewalk a few doors from his home. Two men were arrested and a trial was held, but again, no one was convicted in the second senseless, violent death of a child in the community.

So here we were, a middle school that had lost two students to gun violence only months apart. A little over a month after Ephraim's death, we opened our doors to welcome back students still affected by one death and now mourning a schoolmate who by all rights should have been in a grade seven classroom that day. We used the same display cabinet we'd used for Jordan's memorial to create one for Ephraim, which included his basketball jersey and an airbrushed portrait. To keep his memory alive, we also created the yearly Ephraim Brown Award to honour a sixth-grade student who is a good citizen of Brookview and an exemplary learner. Ephraim's mother, Lorna Brown, came to our assembly honouring her son and the first recipient of the award.

It was impossible for us to make sense of these tragic events, to contemplate the unfulfilled dreams of Jordan and Ephraim. All we could do was to hope for a better tomorrow.

The deaths of Jordan Manners and Ephraim Brown affected me deeply, and left me feeling that Brookview was in urgent need of an intervention. A third event that moved me to make profound changes occurred inside the school, during an assembly. My vice-principal had invited his daughter, a news anchor and host on a local television morning show, to share her story about growing up and living her childhood dream. He was so proud to introduce his daughter to the children gathered in the cafetorium. We had spoken about her many times during the time he was with us, filling in for my permanent vice-principal. Our discussions always connected me back to my five children, as they were conceiving their dreams and working and persevering to fulfill them.

After her proud dad finished, I had the last words. I usually reinforce the importance of sitting, looking and listening. On this day, however, the students sat, hardly looked and refused to listen as our guest presenter began her speech. I made many failing attempts to quiet the students—by asking for their attention with my hand in the air and even by briefly ringing my trusty Belleville cowbell—but nothing worked. It was embarrassing. I knew that they wanted to see me yelling and losing my cool—misery loves company—but on that day, I was not willing to be their dance partner. I finally had to stop the presenter. I thanked her and apologized on behalf of my school. I ordered the students back to their classes and vowed to myself that things would change and must change. As much as I loved my job and I loved the children, I did not love how they were operating. I also didn't love the fact that we as staff were allowing them to get away with behaviour that was so toxic to everything a school is meant to be.

The assembly fiasco took place on a Thursday. By Monday, I was ready to start the morning with an intervention I called Drive for 60. I called it that because 60 percent of our students were achieving at a level below the provincial benchmark. This meant that for every ten students we were teaching, six were not processing information and instructions. When students are not "getting it" in school, they don't get what they should out of life. If the old adage, "The more you learn the more you earn" is true, then more than half of our student population was headed for serious problems. The Drive for 60 intervention was meant to support that adage: learn more to earn more. Students would not only eventually earn financially, but they would quickly earn self-esteem, confidence and happiness.

Monday came and I went to school driving a new bus— the Drive for 60 bus. Students, staff and parents needed to be on that bus. It was the vehicle that would take us from under-achievement and mediocrity to seeing and believing in our potential. Before classes started that morning, I called a Quick Meeting, or a QM. It took place in our main office, with all of the staff gathered around. QMs grew to be part of our culture: anyone could speak, and most did. We always started with refreshments and ended on a good note; we accomplished more in ten to twenty minutes than we did at our two-hour monthly meetings.

At this Monday's QM, I outlined the framework of Drive for 60. The first step concerned the morning routine. We needed to set a good tone for the school day. From now on, a separate entrance would be designated for each of the school's three grades. Staff would meet their students outside, line them up and supervise them as they walked to their lockers. Once the students gathered their materials, they were to be walked quietly to the cafetorium for our morning assembly. In this way, we were sending the students two messages: first, I want to teach you so much that I am coming to get you outside; and second, this is the way we enter the school building and how we get ready for learning.

We started that morning and every morning in the cafetorium. Classes stood in assigned areas, with grade six students at the front and the grade eights at the back. All students were expected to stand and be attentive. This same expectation also carried over into the classroom routine. I had read that standing helps us pay attention and focus better. If you can't focus, you can't learn. The students remained standing through the singing of "O Canada," announcements and my short morning sermon.

Before dismissing students to their classrooms, we had one final piece of business. Students had to repeat after me our new Brookview Middle School credo:

My potential lies inside me.
It gives me the ability
to reach for something,
to become something better.

Then I would continue with the second part:

"I come to school to work hard to be a better person and to be a better student by using the Four T's: Time, Task, Training and Team."

Students had to learn *why* they walked through the school doors every morning. Plus, they needed to know *how* to achieve their goals. What they thought, what they believed and what they did was relevant to the success I wanted for them and the potential I saw in them. Without a belief in their own potential, all effort would be futile. I would tell them that the reason they come to school is to work, to be a better student and to be a better person, and that they were born with the potential to do it. Just set your goal, I would say, believe in your potential and start working.

After an orderly dismissal from the cafetorium, the students were led to their classrooms by the teachers, who started each session with what I call SLICE.

S: standing
L: looking and listening
I: I messages. Students were engaged by asking themselves the following I Messages after the teacher had given them instructions or taught a mini lesson (about twenty minutes): Do I understand the information or instructions? Do I know what to do? Do I have a question?

C: completing the work

E: doing exemplary work

Students were not allowed to sit if they had a question. If teachers were doing their job and knew their students, they would be able to tell who was struggling. Teachers were reminded that six out of ten students were not getting what they were teaching.

SLICE was my main strategy for closing the achievement gap between the 40 percent who were learning up to expectations and the 60 percent who were missing in action during the lesson.

One day during the morning assembly, staff and students were introduced to the Brookview Values. A large mural was painted on one wall in the cafetorium, displaying the values that would govern the behaviour of staff and students: Respect, Responsibility, Organization, Punctuality, Kind and Caring, and High Expectations. During assemblies I would often have hundreds of voices shouting out each value at the same time.

I believe in the adage that our thoughts become our words and our words become our actions, which in turn become our character, then our destiny. Of all the values displayed on that wall, kindness and caring had the greatest impact on the students—they were like the yeast that makes the bread rise. Being kind to the students and demonstrating to them that we cared for them, and about them, raised their confidence and self-esteem.

Even with Drive for 60 in play, things did not always run smoothly. One year, we had a small number of students in grade six over whom we had no influence. They continued to be late every day and, on most days, did no work. They were even breaking into lockers, according to my eyes and ears in the school.

It was on me to address the problem. I had to do something to get them on board. The following September, I started the Gifted Class. We took some of the most challenging seventh-grade students, fifteen in all, and placed them together in one room. The framework for this class was developed around the acronym GIFTED.

G: setting realistic goals and having realistic dreams
I: internal drive and intrinsic motivation
F: fun and joy
T: training to get better.
E: empowerment—taking ownership of their
     learning
D: daily practice.

I selected Darlene Jones to teach this class. This assignment wasn't for everyone, but I believed I had the right teacher to help these students. Darlene had taught successfully for about fifteen years. I had observed her in the classroom many times and had spent a lot of time in conversation with her about teaching and learning. Darlene was a born teacher; I knew she would get to know these students as people, then work to communicate and demonstrate that she cared about them—and she did. (I wasn't the only one who thought Darlene Jones was top-notch. In 2012, her students nominated her for the Toronto Star Teacher of the Year Award, which she won.)

I could not have created a better test for the GIFTED philosophy than with this class. Did it have a positive effect? Only time will tell. All I know is that it was better to try something that might work rather than doing the same things, day in and day out, with the same results. And then people wonder why things don't change.

In 2014, right after returning from Sochi, Russia, with my family—along with P.K. and his gold medal from being a member of the triumphant Canadian men's hockey team—I bumped in to a former student from my Brookview days. We crossed paths in a Canadian Tire store. Soon after saying hello and catching up, I told her that there was a gold medal waiting for her, just like there had been for P.K. "I don't know where it is," I said, "but there is one for you."

If I had to give this student a nickname it would be "Smiley;" I was certain that, every time we met, I'd be greeted with a smile that would make her dentist proud. It turned out, though, that she was just as certain there was no gold medal waiting for her.

My heart sank. Only my belief in her and her youth gave me hope. I hope Smiley and all children will find and discover that thing that they love to do, and be given the opportunity to do it. Only then will they find their gold medal.

When you tell yourself you can't do something, you will be right 100 percent of the time—and you will never grow. Like Smiley, so many children don't see themselves as good enough, big enough, fast enough, strong enough, smart enough, skinny enough or pretty enough. My message to them is this: you might not be good enough right now, but if you work hard enough, persevere enough and pick yourself up every time you fall down, you will get better. My job is to make Smiley and all children feel that they can. It is a long process, not a one-time event.

Drive for 60 was a process with a purpose, and a tool for change and engagement. Student needs are diverse and challenging, and they are becoming greater and more complex. We can't continue to use the same strategies, especially when we can tell they are not working. The program wasn't meant to replace the kind, caring and effective teacher that every student needed in every classroom. I do believe Drive for 60 worked to engage the students. It did not cost any more money to roll out or take extra time in the instructional day. It only required us to think and work differently.

This is where leadership comes into play. In my position at Brookview, I wasn't fearful of failure—my greatest fear was failing to lead. I never saw my job as being that of a manager.

A manager will always take the path laid out before him, one that is well travelled but that might not take him to the desired destination. A leader, on the other hand, is not afraid of clearing the way and breaking a new path. Leading is about thinking outside the box. Brookview needed a new path.

By necessity, a leadership role comes with a certain amount of bureaucracy. This was an aspect of the job I sometimes struggled with—paperwork was not my strong suit, so I delegated most of it and didn't do the rest. Board officials outside of my school seemed more concerned with paper I couldn't find, or didn't return, than with the return on our large investment of education dollars into our children. It's easy for paperwork to get in the way of doing our most important work—the people work. My job as a leader was to get the adults to work in a way that would encourage the children to work better. I gave them Drive for 60. Leaders must find a way to manage bureaucracy, which can distract from the reason we are in our schools every day.

Drive for 60 unified a school that was failing and falling apart. Over time, I started to see some light at the end of the tunnel. Attendance issues were no longer a pressing concern. Students were learning to resolve conflicts peacefully in and around school. Assemblies were more orderly, and students were taking pride in exhibiting positive behaviour.

For example, I shared a new practice for cultivating a kind, peaceful and happy environment. Students were invited to collect as many "thank-yous" as they could each day by doing something kind and caring for someone. Staff was invited to take part too. If you want to be a difference maker, you will do the right thing by extending yourself to others. Any classroom, locker room or boardroom that was punctuated with lots of thank-yous was a good place to be.

When I left Brookview in 2012 after six years as its primary leader, 60 percent of the students were still not achieving at the expected provincial level. A baby learns to crawl, then walk, before she learns how to run. When I started there, Brookview was barely crawling. You could say it was crawling with difficulty. Six years later, the school was walking with some difficulty.

I don't know why I was transferred from Brookview. I would like to think it was for operational reasons. Administrators are generally moved from a school after about five years. This might be a great operational rule for the board, but it is a terrible thing for kids. I did not feel this decision to transfer me was the best thing for the children in my care.

As the American historian Henry Adams put it: "A teacher affects eternity; he can never tell where his influence stops."

In June 2012, I was transferred to Claireville Junior School, a short drive from Brookview, where I worked for one year before retiring in June 2013. I had not been ready to leave Brookview, but I was now ready to leave education. I left Claireville with the memory of a relationship and a moment that encapsulate what I want for my own five children and for every child I worked with.

The story starts on my first day at Claireville, when I was meeting and welcoming everyone back from summer holidays. After the entry bell rang and the students made their way with their teachers to classrooms, one child was clinging to her mother on the sidewalk outside the school. The young girl was transitioning back from summer holidays and from kindergarten to grade one. It was too much change for her. She hugged her mom with all her might. It wasn't long before I had the young student's head on my shoulder, which I believed was made for her, my five children and many more. It is a pillow that children love.

I took her to my office and then convinced her to go to her classroom before morning recess. It was my promise to meet her in the schoolyard during recess that gave her the comfort she was looking for. We met that recess and almost each one after that. She had a routine she liked to follow. It was easy to find me, as I was the tallest tree in the forest of kids running, walking and sitting. She would run to me, touch me with her thigh-high body and run away.

On one particular day, though, she did not run away. Instead, she hovered around me the entire recess. Minutes before the entry bell rang, she told me she had a question she needed to ask that had been bothering her.

Kneeling down, I listened as she whispered in my ear, "Mr. Subban, did the cow really jump over the moon?"

I was not prepared for this question, and I did not immediately know what to say. After a deep breath, followed by a sigh and then a smile, I found what I thought were the right words. "No, the cow didn't jump over the moon . . . but you can reach for the stars."

My job as a parent, coach and educator was to help children believe in their potential and to pave the way for them to reach for the stars. There are billions of stars in our skies. If you reach high enough, you are bound to touch one. And it is only when you are reaching for something that you become something and someone better.

1 2

The Subban Hat Trick

On June 30, 2013, Maria, Taz, Tasha, P.K., Malcolm, Jordan and I were gathered at Prudential Center, home of the NHL's New Jersey Devils. But no hockey was being played on this early summer day. There wasn't a skate, helmet or shin guard in sight. It was the annual NHL draft day, and the uniform was a suit and tie.

Between the NHL and the OHL, Maria and I have experienced six draft days. They are transformative days. Lifelong dreams come true, or are crushed. Careers of fame and fortune begin, or never get off the ground. These days are filled with anxiety and waiting. Lots of waiting. As a player, there is only one thing you want: to hear your name called. The round in which it is called isn't important. In that cavernous arena—and on live television—before thousands of players, parents, executives, coaches, agents and journalists, all that matters is to hear an NHL general manager say your name.

The name we wanted to hear read from the podium on this particular day was "Jordan Subban." The pressure on Jordan, an undersized eighteen-year-old defenceman with the Belleville Bulls, was tremendous. Six years earlier, in 2007, P.K. had been drafted in the second round, forty-third overall, by the Montreal Canadiens. At the age of twenty-four, he was already a star in the NHL. In fact, just a few weeks earlier, P.K. had won the Norris Trophy as the league's top defenceman. And just a year earlier, Malcolm, as a nineteen-year-old goalie, had been drafted by the Boston Bruins in the first round, twenty-fourth overall. Jordan was expected to be chosen in the third or fourth round.

Hockey, like most sports, is filled with rituals. One of those rituals is to wear a suit and tie on draft day. And for the Subbans, it is not just any suit and tie—it has to be custom-made. This family tradition started with P.K.'s draft, and had its origins with the Belleville Bulls. George Burnett, the Bull's coach and general manager, along with his coaching staff, made sure our boys and the other players knew how to conduct themselves, both on and off the ice. If you turned on the TV and one of George's boys was being interviewed, he was wearing a suit. Mind you, since those Belleville days, P.K. has taken this ritual to another level. He had his own personal tailor in Montreal, has an endorsement deal with clothier R.W & Co., and in 2016 was named one of Canada's best-dressed by *Hello!* magazine. My former neighbour and long-time friend Dennis has a saying about life: "Half of it is how you look." I'm still waiting for him to tell me what the other half is.

For P.K.'s draft day, we took him to Caruso Fine Tailoring on Danforth Avenue in Toronto's Greektown and had a suit made. This is the one time I don't mind my children wearing designer clothing. It's their big moment; they are on hockey's biggest stage, for everyone to see. You want to make a great first impression and look your best so you can feel your best. We bought P.K. his draft-day suit, and when it was Malcolm's turn, P.K. brought him to Montreal. He bought his brother's draft-day suit from his own tailor. For Jordan, we went back to Caruso.

Draft day may come across as an event, but I see it as part of a process. Our kids have been working for this day since they started out in hockey. I compare it to signing up for a course. You register, do all the assignments and then there is a big final exam you must take to get your grade. And that is what the draft is. You don't know what the grade is going to be, but you know you are going to be given a number. In this case, the lower the number you receive, the better you will be looked upon that day. But that number is only a draft number—it's not pinned to the back of you for the rest of your life.

On draft day you must sit and wait to get your mark. Each second is like an hour. Emotions are high, and there is no way to avoid that if you are the parent of a player. Your son has written that exam, and you can't help but want him to get a good grade.

The wait to hear your child's name feels like the longest of your life. It takes everything out of you. You wait and wait and wait—hoping for a huge weight to be lifted from your shoulders. You don't care *when* you hear it, you just want to hear it.

When were we going to hear it on this day? Who was going to take Jordan? What if we didn't hear his name? There are no guarantees on draft day.

Jordan didn't have as much support in the stands on draft day as his brothers had. He was allowed to sit only with Maria and me—his agent was nearby, and his brothers and sisters were seated across the arena. P.K. and Malcolm had had all their siblings with them, but this year organizers wanted to speed up the process by minimizing the hugs and kisses before the players walked up to the stage.

After thirty selections, the first round was over. Jordan's name had not been called, but his good friend Max Domi's had. The son of Maple Leafs legend Tie Domi was selected twelfth overall by the Phoenix Coyotes.

In the second round, the tension was mounting and Jordan was starting to get emotional. And then, unexpectedly, Max came over and sat down beside Jordan. At one point, Jordan put his head on Max's shoulder.

It was Max's moment. He had been taken in the first round, and he could have been celebrating with his friends and parents. Instead, he came over to sit with his buddy and offer his shoulder when Jordan needed it. What a nice thing to do. It's one of the life lessons I have tried to teach my children and my students: if you see someone in need of help, step forward. Max showed that it's not always about what you get, but what you give.

Thirty-one more picks and round two passed. We did not hear Jordan's name. The tension grew. Then the third round.

Thirty more picks. On to round four. We were now at the twentieth pick of round four, and teams were choosing defencemen, but not Jordan. Then, at 9:39 p.m., with the twenty-fourth pick of the fourth round, the words we were longing to hear passed through General Manager Mike Gillis's lips: "The Vancouver Canucks select from Belleville of the Ontario Hockey League, Jordan Subban." Relief. The weight, that immense weight, lifted. Then joy and hugs and a few tears. The young defenceman with the Belleville Bulls—my son, my third son and my fifth child—was the 115th selection of the day. Jordan heard his name. We all heard his name.

It didn't sink in immediately, but I soon realized my family had accomplished a rare feat. I call it the Subban Hat Trick: all three of my boys have been drafted by NHL teams. I was born in Jamaica, Maria in Montserrat. Neither of us played organized hockey, nor did anyone else in our families. We are not a family with a hockey pedigree. So many hockey parents dream of having one son drafted by an NHL team. We now had three. It is an accomplishment of which we as parents are extremely proud.

It was a tremendous accomplishment for Jordan, obviously. Here are his recollections of that momentous day.

JORDAN

It feels like a long time ago. I had no idea where I was going to go. The wait for me was three hours, but it must have felt like twenty. I was getting nervous, but once my name was called, I was never in so much shock. I was like, "Wait . . . what? Who picked me?" I was zoned out. I didn't hear the name of the team. I just heard "Jordan Subban," and my head went up. I saw Vancouver. A Canadian team. This is crazy.

I've never been so happy in my life. I jumped out of my seat, hugged my parents and rushed down to the stage as quickly as I could to meet everyone and shake their hands and tell them how excited I was to be a Vancouver Canuck.

The second and third round was where I figured I would go. When the second round passed, I was getting nervous. When the third round was starting, I was getting really, really nervous. During the fourth round, my agent, Mark Guy, was there with me, saying it was going to be soon, and I always trusted him. You are nervous and do start to get those thoughts you might not get picked, but once I was selected, it was all over, and I was so happy to be part of an NHL organization.

Max Domi and I have been best buddies for as long as I can remember. We grew up playing hockey together. To this day we still hang out. I appreciated him coming over. You expect your family to be there. He didn't have to be.

My OHL draft experience was a little different. I was the fifth-overall pick to Belleville. I went up that day and did a press conference. I waited five minutes, ten minutes, before I was picked. I know some players in my OHL draft who were fourth-, fifth-, sixth-rounders and turned out to be great OHL players, so that became my goal [after the NHL draft]: to be one of those guys who was picked in the fourth round and prove I can make it.

The odds against making it in the NHL are great, to say the least. Hockey is like a religion in Canada. Millions of kids skate. Hundreds of thousands of children play hockey. Consider them the base of the pyramid, and making it to the NHL the tip. You have better odds of winning the lottery than reaching the top of that pyramid and making a living playing in the NHL. As you move up the pyramid, as you climb up the hockey mountain, there are fewer and fewer players at each competitive level. If you reach the major junior level you are a talented player. This is a great accomplishment. But those teenagers still have only a 5 percent chance of making it to the NHL. Talented athletes from Russia, the United States, Sweden, Germany, Austria, Switzerland, Denmark, Norway, Latvia, Slovakia, Croatia, the Czech Republic and Finland are playing competitive hockey and training hard to earn a place in the league.

In the recent book *Selling the Dream*, hockey journalist Ken Campbell and co-author Jim Parcels looked at a 1985 study of all ten-year-old hockey players in Ontario. There were twenty-two thousand boys playing organized hockey in Canada's largest province. Of those players, 110 made it to the OHL while another twenty-two earned scholarships to Division 1 schools in the United States. So, 132 of twenty-two thousand players earned spots on teams in the top leagues that feed the NHL. Of those 132 players, only seven went on to play in the NHL.

Looking at other data from Ontario, the authors found that for any age group, about twenty-five thousand boys will register to play hockey in the province. Of that number, about twenty-five will go on to play at least one NHL game. These odds are a staggeringly low 1 in one thousand.

The Subban Hat Trick was cause to celebrate, but, of course, getting drafted and making it in the NHL are two different things. P.K. made it, but what if Jordan does not become an NHL player?

There's one message I keep coming back to with Jordan: never count him out. And that is not just my assessment. Consider what his brothers and sisters have to say about him.

In 2012, Neate Sager of Yahoo! Sports interviewed Malcolm.

He said, "One of the popular questions at NHL scouting combine interviews in recent years has been, 'If your city was invaded and you could get all of your family out except for one person, who would you leave behind?' Between your parents, sisters, P.K., your younger brother, who would stay back, or do you know the answer the NHL teams are looking for?"

Here was Malcolm's answer: "It'd be hard, but I would probably say my younger brother Jordan. He's the most ruthless and relentless out of any of us. He'd be able to survive the best out of any of us, so if I had to leave anyone behind, it'd probably be him."

TAZ

Taz: Yeah, he's a fighter. My mom will say that. His birth story. He had asthma and had to be on steroids. The doctors, when they found out she was pregnant . . .

Tasha: They wanted her to have an abortion.

Taz: Because they said his chance of having a life were slim to none. Mom had really high blood pressure and it was an issue with the meds. She said, "Whatever's to be, will be." She had him, and she's always said Jordan is a fighter.

Tasha: If the world was coming to a crumble and we couldn't find Jordan, we would be worried, but at the same time . . .

Taz: He doesn't need much. He really doesn't need much.

Tasha: It would be Jordan who would be the fighter. Like Dad always says, "Jordan—it doesn't matter, he's going to get what he wants."

Taz: Jordan is very strong. He can take certain things.

Tasha: He can't take teasing, though. That's actually his weak point. He will fight. I have seen P.K. and him get it on.

Taz: Yeah, that's the thing with boys, though. Then they'll laugh about it.

TASHA

P.K.

I'm very proud of my brothers. We've all worked hard. We've all been successful in our own ways, but you are only going to get back what you give. So I always tell them, "Nothing is given. Nothing is guaranteed. You've got to go work and get it." They still have a long way to go to get to the NHL, but they are on the path, and how hard they work will determine whether they get there or not.

13

The Dream Becomes a Reality

Maria and I have lived in Canada for forty-seven of the country's 150 years, and like so many Canadian parents, our hopes for ourselves and our children have been built on dreams. This great country has given my family the opportunity to have those dreams; it has made us who we are, and I hope the work and passions of the Subbans have helped to make Canada better.

One of those passions, of course, is hockey—a game that is loved and played from coast to coast to coast by young and old, by girls and boys. The only thing that separates my family from the majority of Canadians playing hockey is the colour of our skin.

Maria and I passed our love for the game on to our children, but I never imagined we would one day turn on the television set and watch one of *our sons* playing for the Montreal Canadiens against the Toronto Maple Leafs, two of the Original Six teams.

Is it a moment like this when the NHL dream was fulfilled for Team Subban? Was it when the boys were drafted to the National Hockey League? Was it signing that NHL contract? It's like buying your first home: once you sign the papers, it is yours. Those are all special moments, but personally, I felt that my boys had made it the second the freshly sharpened blades of their skates cut across the pristine ice for their first NHL exhibition games.

The dream became a reality for P.K. during his second training camp with the Montreal Canadiens. On September 24, 2008, he was scheduled to play in his first pre-season game in Detroit against the defending Stanley Cup champions. Maria and I made the four-hour drive so we could witness our oldest son wearing an NHL jersey for the first time on the ice. We left Toronto with plenty of time to spare. However, we almost did not make it to the dream game.

As we came off Highway 401 in Windsor and took the tunnel under the Detroit River into downtown Detroit, our car was selected out of the long lineup for a random inspection. The U.S. border agent appeared dressed for war, and he had a dog that was sniffing everything around us. The agent was looking through my overnight bag when he found an unmarked pill bottle with some codeine I was taking for pain from an injury sustained in an automobile accident. I had left the prescription bottle at home and placed a few in the unmarked container. The border agent explained the law to me, saying I could be arrested and charged with trafficking a narcotic. Luckily, all I got was a stern warning and a lesson learned.

We drove on to Joe Louis Arena, but our attention and focus had been hijacked by the scare at the border. It was getting darker too, making it more difficult to find our way. We gradually regained our composure, got our bearings and made it to the game just in time to witness P.K. as he stepped onto the ice for his first NHL game.

That small step for P.K. was a giant one for Team Subban, especially for Malcolm and Jordan, as P.K. left his blade marks for them to follow. What I remember about that game is that P.K. did not look out of place. I couldn't believe my eyes—there was our little P.K., playing on NHL ice alongside some of the greatest hockey players in the world. Once his blade carved into the frozen surface, he was like a fish in water. He looked just the way he did when he first played house league for the Flames at Chris Tonks Arena in the City of York.

The NHL dream is one example of a big dream. Big dreams require lots of time to pursue; they are costly and a great distance away. They take time and effort to make real. You can't speed up time, but you can get to work with a focus on becoming better. The important thing is to use the time to make yourself better. If P.K. had not made time to train and to do his hockey tasks he would not have had the opportunity to step on the ice in Joe Louis Arena.

Society is hard on our children today. The Internet and social media can be endlessly distracting and can serve to distance children from the guidance of their parents. And as the breakdown of family structures becomes more common, it has made life a lot more challenging for our children. Chasing a dream, a big dream, can give children focus and discipline and support the development of important skills they need to navigate life's experiences and challenges. It is so easy to give up on a dream that is far away, which is why you must find a way to make achieving it part of your daily experience. Your children need you to be a teacher and a coach, but ultimately it is your love and emotional support that is their security blanket. If they don't feel safe and secure they will be paralyzed by fear and will not take risks. Fear of failure is one of the most powerful of dream killers.

As the boys were progressing through minor hockey, I always emphasized that achieving a milestone does not guarantee you have "made it"—even on that day you hit the NHL ice for the first time. What you learn is that there is a price tag attached to your successes and achievements, and you must continue to pay the price every day for your dream. You just never know the exact amount of effort, practice, training and determination that is required. Doing your best is only good for today. You must pay again tomorrow.

P.K. charted the course for his brothers to follow. He was the first one in our family to travel the hockey journey. He faced strong headwinds, but in the process he created a tailwind for Malcolm and Jordan. They knew what to do, how to do it and how long to do it. Translated, that means they knew the importance of practising in the short term, training for the long haul and always working to be better.

The dream, at times, did not look too realistic for Malcolm, especially when he moved from being a player to being a goalie at the age of twelve. In the view of some people, he went from being a very good prospect as a defenceman to having zero chance of making it to the NHL as a goalie. But Malcolm believed he could do it, and he was willing to put in the work. That work paid off when he was drafted by the Boston Bruins twenty-fourth overall in the first round in 2012. It wasn't long before Malcolm played his first game in the NHL—against his older brother.

Malcolm's first exhibition game was against the Canadiens in Montreal on September 16, 2013. I had imagined such a game, but I'd never dared to hope it would happen this early. I had already lived one of my dreams: for P.K. to play for my favourite team, the Montreal Canadiens. Now I was about to live a second dream: watching the boys compete against each other in an NHL game. It was determined by the team that Malcolm would make his debut during the second half of the game. All the fans around us knew the situation, and it seemed as if they were waiting with us for the big moment. I didn't know how it would all unfold, but one thing I knew for certain is that Maria couldn't wait to sing "Holy Moly, What a Goalie." I am certain that when she did, Malcolm heard her voice.

Malcolm entered the game partway through and stopped all twelve shots he faced, even one from P.K. The Bruins won, 6–3. The headline on the Canadian Press story read, "Malcolm Subban tops brother P.K. as Bruins down Canadiens." P.K. scored a goal against Bruins goaltender Chad Johnson in the second period, but he didn't get much on his shot against his younger brother.

"I think he had one that was probably his slowest shot ever, just a little knuckle-puck on net, but it was pretty fun," Malcolm was quoted as saying.

"It was a pretty cool experience," P.K. told reporters. "We made eye contact, but we lost the game, so I'm not going to smile or talk to him too much . . . I thought he handled himself well for his first game."

My heart was happy that night, especially for Malcolm, who had come so far in a short period of time. Being a Canadiens fan meant I'd never liked the Bruins growing up, but I had to change my affiliation. Move over P.K. and the Habs—the Bruins and Malcolm now had a piece of my heart.

A year later, on September 23, 2014, Jordan Subban stepped on the ice to play his first game in the NHL at Rogers Arena in Vancouver, British Columbia. As luck would have it, I was in Vancouver working as an ambassador for Hyundai's Hockey Helpers program. This was my third first game, and it came with the same mix of happiness and nervous tension. I was anxious as I waited for Jordan to step onto the ice. He didn't start the game and had to wait his turn on the bench, but I knew his chance would come. Suddenly, there he was. And it wasn't long into his first shift, in his very first game, that Jordan scored on a screened shot from the blue line. His coaches and teammates did a great job in supporting him, and they all assisted on his first goal.

Jordan came to see me after the game in an area designated for family and friends. He couldn't wait to see me, and I couldn't wait to see him. He lived his dream and made me so proud. I flew back to Toronto the next day and, shortly afterward, Jordan returned to Belleville to play his final season with the Bulls.

Jordan's first-game story did not end with the final buzzer at the end of third period, however. When Jordan scored, a photograph of him celebrating with his teammates was posted on a newspaper website. The caption mentioned the names of the two players flanking him, but described Jordan as the "dark guy in the middle." An uproar ensued on social media, and the newspaper apologized for publishing the caption. I wasn't aware reporters were waiting for Jordan as he landed at Toronto Pearson International Airport. I took pride in how Jordan dealt with this distraction, saying on television that he had put the matter behind him.

"I had a chance to talk with a representative of the paper," Jordan told reporters. "It seemed like a pretty honest mistake. Am I worried about it? No. If people should be talking about something, it should be the way I played last night rather than that. Hopefully, it will just die down."

I was proud of his first goal and more proud of the way he dealt with the adversity he was facing. He saw it as a distraction and was not willing to give it permission to keep him from being a big leaguer.

Life is good to you when you find your passion and make it work for you. In turn, you must be good to life. One way to be good to life is to use your blessings to help others. Many elite athletes have used their wealth and fame to support worthy causes at home and abroad. I like to think P.K. has raised the bar a little in this regard.

In 2010, an earthquake that measured 7.0 on the Richter scale rocked Haiti, causing widespread devastation and killing

220,000 people. More than 300,000 were injured. One year later, working through the National Hockey League Players' Association, P.K. had an opportunity to visit the Caribbean nation with World Vision to give a helping hand and offer moral support. P.K. played road hockey with the children, which gave them an opportunity to smile and have fun.

P.K. was twenty-one when he went to Haiti. My words to him before he flew there were: "P.K., you are now playing in the NHL and are making it in your profession. This is a great opportunity for you to start making it in your life." I wasn't sure if he knew what I meant, or what he needed to do to have a meaningful and purposeful life. His trip to Haiti was an opportunity for him to engage in some soul-searching.

After he returned, P.K. said visiting Haiti had a profound impact on him. He saw just how fortunate he was compared to the people there: families were lost, homes were lost—even hope was lost.

Fast forward to September 2015. P.K. had already made his mark on the ice; he'd been awarded a Norris Trophy for the league's top defenceman, and had also become one of the league's top earners. P.K. felt there was no better moment to give back to the city where his N.H.L. career began, and no better cause than one that would benefit kids. At a public event, P.K. announced his pledge to raise $10 million over seven years for Montreal Children's Hospital (MCH). It was the largest charitable donation by an athlete in Canadian history. P.K. has scored many goals on the ice for his hockey teams; however, it was his goal off the ice that had the world cheering the loudest.

Maria and I flew into Montreal the day before the announcement, which had been in the planning stages since the spring and was finalized in August. I was not expecting the degree of media attention when we went to the hospital the next day. As we came to the atrium where the announcement was going to take place, people had already started arriving. Then more people came, and then even more people. The place was packed. I saw swarms of reporters, photographers and TV cameras.

Seated to my right was Jean Béliveau's widow, Élise Béliveau. While we were waiting for P.K. to speak, I told her about the time I'd met her husband in Toronto, when he sat with me while we both watched a ten-year-old P.K. play. Now she was sitting with me to listen to P.K. speak—unbelievable. Her husband was not only a great hockey player, with many Stanley Cup rings to show for his mastery on the ice, but he was also well known for his charitable work.

Suddenly, a buzzer sounded. It was time to drop the puck. Michel Lacroix, the public-address announcer from the Montreal Canadiens, was the master of ceremonies. He spoke in French and introduced everyone.

My eyes misted over when P.K. walked into the atrium to take his position on stage and the crowd chanted, "P.K.! P.K.!" I don't think I have shed any better tears.

Next, hospital dignitaries spoke: people from the board of directors and from the fundraising foundation. Also on the program was P.K.'s sister, Taz, who serves as a director with the P.K. Subban Foundation; on this day, her job was to discuss the foundation's mission and goals. Part of the ceremony involved revealing that the 486-square-metre, three-storey atrium we were sitting in had been renamed the Atrium P.K. Subban.

Then it was P.K.'s turn. There was a lot of noise and then his big smile. Walking up to the podium, P.K. was his usual self, slapping hands with patients. P.K. may be a star player in National Hockey League, but at the hospital, it is the parents and their sick children who are the stars and all-stars. Some of these all-stars were in wheelchairs, in regular chairs or in the arms of comforting parents and hospital staff. They were all dressed differently: either in hockey jerseys, hospital clothes or street clothes—but all were wearing smiles just as big as P.K.'s. Everyone had gathered to see the sports star, but they were the ones shining so bright on him.

When P.K. spoke, it was in French. I was so impressed. Mrs. Béliveau said to me, "I can't believe how well he is speaking French. It's like he speaks French." P.K. was reading his presentation, but it came across naturally, as if from the top of his head. Then P.K. began telling stories in English. I was amazed with his storytelling, and I told him so afterward. It's those stories people are able to connect with. His stories communicated to us the reason why he is doing what he is doing.

Here is part of his speech that day:

> When I first spoke to the Children's Hospital about this opportunity, I thought to myself, "What's authentic?" because the way I play the game, it's me; the way I talk, it's me, it's my family; the way I walk, the way I dress, it's me. You're not getting somebody else; you're getting P.K.—all the time. Sometimes that gets me into trouble, but . . . I thought about the fact that I always wanted to do something special and something significant, but, like anything else, you have to take baby steps to get there. For the past five years I have experimented with myself, quietly in some ways . . . going to the hospital on

Christmas morning my first year in the NHL with Ray Lalonde, who at the time worked with the marketing department. No cameras, no nothing like that, just to figure out what I wanted to do.

. . . In life I believe you are not defined by what you accomplish but by what you do for others. That's how I have lived my life. This is not about hockey; this is not about how many goals I score next year, even how the team does. For me, this is about how I live my life; this is about what is important in life in general, and I think sometimes I try to think, "P.K., are you a hockey player or are you just someone who plays hockey?" I just play hockey. I just play hockey. Because one day I won't be playing hockey anymore. I'll just be someone who played hockey. So what do I want people to remember me for other than being a hockey player? Well, every time you walk into this hospital, you'll know what I stand for.

I can't take the credit for what P.K. has done. I would be lying to myself to say his generosity and desire to help others came solely from me and Maria. There are many people who had a hand in creating P.K. Subban. It goes back to the village it takes to raise a child. There are so many people who have interacted with P.K., and so many people he respects and looks up to, not just his parents. I would like to think that the team of people around him has had an influence on who he is today. Obviously, parents are the first teachers; home is the first school. But he needed to attend other schools.

Belleville was where the boys were first introduced to community service. For all of the Bulls players—especially the ones who had finished high school and were only taking one credit at the community college—it was a big part of their responsibilities. The players would go to schools and hospitals and work with seniors. They were learning important values.

At P.K.'s minor midget banquet, David Branch, the commissioner of the OHL and CHL, told us that playing hockey in the OHL is not a privilege but an opportunity. That thinking behind that statement is now very clear to me. The OHL provides not only an opportunity to be a better hockey player, but also to be a better young person. You can only achieve that through how you treat others.

P.K. had fame and fortune at twenty-six years of age, with a lot of time on his hands in the off-season. He wasn't ready to start a family, which would have certainly occupied his extra time. Instead, he took a different route. P.K. donated some of his money to the Children's Hospital, but mostly what he committed to was to donate his time: fundraising, doing public relations and making goodwill visits.

I think it's safe to say I was surprised at how proud I was of P.K. that day. First of all, I didn't know his generosity would resonate with so many people. Someone sent Natasha a report of all the media that ran the story, and it was unbelievable. P.K.'s pledge made headlines not just in Canada but around the world.

Like many professional athletes, P.K. has visited hospitals in various cities to spend time with young children who are recuperating from an illness or fighting just to make it through the day or night. Many of P.K.'s visits are not publicized. I was speaking recently to a father whose daughter, who was about six, had been a cancer patient at Montreal Children's Hospital.

He told me P.K. came to the hospital one Christmas morning with gifts for the children. There were no cameras or reporters. His wife had spent the night there with their daughter. He said P.K.'s kindness and thoughtfulness brought tears of joy to her eyes.

P.K.'s trade from Montreal to Nashville will not affect his commitment to MCH, and he is also exploring ways to help sick children in his new hockey home. The visits to Montreal Children's Hospital may not be as frequent, but his passion for the hospital and the children will not wane.

There was another unexpected and gratifying side-effect of P.K.'s generosity: in March of 2017, P.K. was honoured by Governor General David Johnston with a Meritorious Service Decoration, created by Queen Elizabeth to recognize Canadians for their exceptional service to our country. P.K.'s boyhood dream was to play hockey in the National Hockey League. Who would have thought that fulfilling his dream would create a spider's web connecting him to a bigger goal—giving back to the city of Montreal and our country through his philanthropy. It is P.K.'s elite hockey skills that have allowed my oldest son to be a difference maker—on and off the ice.

14

Eyes on the Prize

In late January 2016, Maria and I were in Grenada with our friends Sally and Ron, who had built their dream home on a hill overlooking the Caribbean Sea. (As much as I have always embraced Canadian winters, there's something to be said for a dose of Caribbean sunshine during those months, and now that I am no longer tied to the school calendar I like to exchange my skates for swimwear any chance I can get.)

During our vacation, Jordan returned to Toronto during the AHL all-star break. We live a four-hour drive from Utica, close enough for Jordan and his teammate to make a quick visit. Jordan loves driving my truck when he comes home, and he had it all to himself while I was away. Although he knows where to find my keys, he did ask permission to take the truck out that evening. Jordan was by himself as he drove on Toronto's busy Gardiner Expressway, heading downtown to meet some friends. It was early in the evening and quickly getting dark when a rear tire blew and separated from the rim, making the truck difficult to drive and giving Jordan a scare. I don't know how he managed to control the vehicle and then manoeuvre it safely away from the cars around him and the guardrails. To make matters worse, there was hardly any shoulder on which he could pull over and park. It was an accident scene waiting for another accident to happen. After turning on the hazards and calling 911, Jordan instinctively dialled my number to tell me he was okay.

What you need to understand about Jordan is that he wears his emotions on his sleeve, and he doesn't like to be late, so when he called with the news about the blown tire, I knew he was a bit anxious. When it comes to knowing our children, Maria and I are always on the same wavelength. Maria advised him to call our former neighbour Dennis, who would come and be Jordan's surrogate parent during this mishap. Jordan was lucky. The police said the truck could have easily rolled into traffic, and who knows how that might have turned out. With the support of the police, a tow truck driver, and Dennis, Jordan was eventually on the road again.

I was surprised the tire had come apart; I had bought those tires only a few months earlier. When I returned home I saw the tire in the garage. The remains of it looked like cooked spaghetti noodles wrapped around an almost naked rim.

Two weeks later, on Saturday, February 6, we were still in Grenada enjoying the magical view from Ron and Sally's elevated veranda. At 7 p.m., I brought up Jordan's Utica home game on my iPad, and at 7:30, I also tuned in to watch Malcolm's game, which was in Portland, Maine. That game had just started when I heard one of the play-by-play announcers say that Malcolm had suffered an injury during the pre-game skate and had been taken to the hospital. One moment I had been hypnotized by the view of acres of green with the blue ocean behind, and the next minute, that beauty disappeared. I momentarily forgot where I was while urgent questions flooded my mind. What had happened to Malcolm? How serious was his injury? What could we do when we were so far away?

I called both Taz and Tasha to see if they had news for us, but they were learning about Malcolm's injury for the first time from me. My next call was to Newport Sports, the agency that represents all our boys. Agent Mark Guy was not aware of the injury but went to work right away to find out everything he could. That night we went to bed with some lingering questions and the intention to get ourselves to Malcolm's hospital bed as soon as possible.

Malcolm's injury, as it turned out, was quite serious. During warm-up, a puck had crushed his larynx, and if he hadn't received immediate medical treatment at the arena his airway would have swollen shut. Malcolm was not in the habit of wearing a Patrick Roy–style neck guard, and he hadn't been on this day. Malcolm later told us he had trouble breathing during those anxious moments. He tried to shake it off, and when he couldn't work through it, he knew he had a major problem.

That night, a tube was placed in his throat to allow him to breathe and to stabilize him for his ride in an ambulance to Boston, where two days later he endured an operation that lasted between four and five hours. Taz and Tasha flew to Boston on Sunday to be with their brother. Taz said it was the longest day of her life. It was agonizing for us as well as we could not leave Grenada till Monday, the day he was to have surgery.

As our Air Canada plane taxied down the runway in Grenada, Maria snuck in a last-second phone call to Tasha to get feedback from Malcolm's throat surgeon. We prayed there would be some news to share, as we did not want to be in the air not knowing Malcolm's condition. Happily, word came just as the plane's engines were roaring for takeoff and everyone was buckled into their seats: Malcolm would be okay and was expected to have a full recovery.

The next day we were on another plane, finally en route to Boston. The Bruins took care of our travel arrangements to Boston General Hospital where Malcolm was convalescing. The boys have dental and medical coverage through their teams and hockey leagues, so we never had to worry about who was paying—we only had to worry if he would be healthy enough to speak or play goal again. I knew Malcolm also would be concerned about his singing voice, since music-making is one of his passions.

We couldn't wait to see our son. I knew he had the same emotions bundled up inside him as he lay immobile in his hospital bed. I greeted Malcolm the same way I did the day he was born, on December 21, 1993, by hugging him gently and kissing him on his forehead. The doctor had instructed Malcolm not to try to speak, even though I believed and hoped he still

had the ability. (Of course, Malcolm isn't much of a talker any-
way, so I knew keeping quiet wouldn't be a problem for him.)
On that first day after surgery, he improvised a kind of sign
language to communicate, which we adapted to quickly.

On Wednesday, two days after his operation and four days
after the injury, the doctors sent Malcolm home to the house he
was renting with a Providence teammate and his wife. His room-
mate had been called up to the parent club early in the season,
so there was room for Maria and me to spend a little over a week
with him as he recovered. Over the following weeks and months,
he began talking normally again and got back to playing hockey.
His singing voice, however, was affected and will not fully
recover due to permanent damage to his vocal cords.

We are so thankful for the Bruins organization, Boston
General Hospital, and the medical team who worked together
to restore Malcolm's health so he could resume the pursuit of
his dream. And it goes without saying that, these days, he is
never without a neck guard when he's on the ice.

Injury is a reality of sports. There are the emotional injuries
wrapped up in losses, which are common to the sporting arena.
Those injuries sting you like a bee, and only playing and winning the next game can take away that pain. However, a physical
injury is something altogether different. You often don't know
when you will play your next game—if ever.

A month after Malcolm's scare, Team Subban achieved a
new kind of hat trick: a mishap hat trick. On Thursday, March
10, in the blink of an eye, P.K. had an awkward collision with
teammate Alexei Emelin's butt during the third period of a
home game against the Buffalo Sabres and fell to the ice. After
being treated by medics for several minutes, he had to be carried

away on a stretcher. This time, Maria and I were in Turks and Caicos. We were not watching the game that night, so we didn't see the collision, and only heard about it when Taz called to tell us that P.K. had suffered a neck injury. Mark Guy called immediately afterward to give us the full briefing.

The injury, which prevented P.K. from turning his neck side to side, was serious enough that he had to miss the remaining fourteen games of the season. What none of us could have known then was that the night of the collision would be the last time our son would wear a Montreal Canadiens jersey in an NHL game. There was no post-season play for Montreal that year, and P.K. would need a big chunk of the off-season to get over his butt-to-head injury. The summer of 2016 was the longest he had ever been sidelined from the ice or the gym. He was like a duck out of water, growing impatient with the mandated resting and healing. P.K. knows the importance of training, and was frustrated he couldn't do any until the injury healed. He learned a valuable lesson that summer: even though one challenge may be dealt with, another will come and take its place.

The start of 2016 brought to mind the well-known curse, "May you live in interesting times." Only three months in and we'd had to deal with a disintegrating tire, a puck to the throat, and now an injury that had sidelined P.K. for the rest of the regular season. But the next three months would also contain their share of interesting times—and the Subban name would dominate international hockey headlines for some time to come. So far, our hockey journey had taken us from arenas to hospitals.

Now it was about to take us to a part of the game that only fans love—trades.

There had been persistent rumours all spring and early summer that P.K. might be traded. On Wednesday, June 29, just two days before July 1—when P.K.'s no-trade clause would have come into effect—and two years into an eight-year contract with the Canadiens, P.K. was traded to the Nashville Predators in exchange for Predators captain and all-star defenceman Shea Weber.

I was not surprised when I found out. When I think about my emotional state regarding P.K.'s trade, I liken it to the experience of bringing home a new baby. You love the new baby, but its arrival doesn't change your love for the children you already have. The Canadiens were the team that drafted P.K., allowing him to live his dream to play hockey "like those guys on TV." He had played more than four hundred games in the NHL at the time of his trade, but his dream to play in the NHL and win a Stanley Cup was still very much alive. It still is. But these days, he's pursuing that dream in Nashville.

It is October 14, 2016, and the soft rain that's falling on Nashville ahead of Opening Night hasn't dampened the spirits of the fans pouring into Bridgestone Arena to watch the Predators take on their archrivals, the Chicago Blackhawks.

The Blackhawks get on the board early in the first period and Nashville is trailing, 0–1. But five minutes later, Chicago defenceman Brian Campbell is called for interference against Nashville centre Colton Sissons, and the Predators are on the power play with a man advantage. P.K. Subban is roaming the blue line; the puck is being passed around, the Predators looking for the right shot. P.K. passes to forward Ryan Johansen, who holds the puck for a moment before flipping it back to P.K., who winds up for one of his trademark slapshots. BOOM! The puck rockets past screened Chicago netminder Corey Crawford into the back of the net. The goal horn blares, and fans leap to their feet waving their yellow Opening Night commemorative towels. At 7:46 in the first period of his first game with Nashville, on his first shot on net wearing his new gold Predator's uniform, P.K. tied the game.

As the TV announcer said, "Well, you can't script it any better than this." One fan tweeted that the roar from the sold-out crowd of 17,256 fans that night was the loudest he had ever heard in Bridgestone Arena. And since I was part of that crowd, I may have to take some credit.

Maria and I wouldn't have missed P.K.'s first game with Nashville for anything, and we were proud to wear our gold No. 76 Subban jerseys for the first time along with our son.

That first goal was important: P.K. needed to make his mark early. In his post-game comments with reporters, P.K. said he wasn't even thinking of scoring a goal in his first game with the Predators. It was his first meaningful game in seven months, since his neck injury on March 10. "I just wanted to kind of get back into it, to get my feet under me and play hard and play physical, just try and do what the coaching staff asks me to do."

The stakes were high in Nashville; the team had lost in seven games to the San Jose Sharks in the Western Conference semifinals in May. The trade of two of the NHL's star defencemen was still being talked about months after it all went down. In a promo for *Hockey Night in Canada* that week, Don Cherry said he was going to reveal the reason for the trade. *Sports Illustrated* made the trade the focus of its NHL season preview article. During his time with the Habs, P.K. had had his detractors, but they are nothing compared to his passionate fans, who vented their feelings on social media.

Maybe it's because the Canadiens were my team for so many years, but I still feel Montreal is the most special place to witness an NHL game. It's hard to describe. For me, Montreal has represented the essence of the game: Original Six hockey. But once inside Bridgestone Arena with Maria, I came to the realization that Nashville was my new team. Sitting in that arena for the first time, with the live music playing during breaks and at each intermission, the pulsing crowd wearing their gold jerseys and hats, I realized this is hockey too. You wouldn't know you were in Nashville, south of the Mason-Dixon line—you felt you were in an authentic hockey town. Because you were.

Each arena has its own personality. In Nashville, you can feel every moment. You are aware of the speed of the game and the size of the players, who appear to make the ice surface seem smaller. And there doesn't seem to be a bad seat in the house. The Predators put in a lot of effort to make the game experience fun for the fans. They have cheerleaders dancing in the aisles; figure skaters carve out turns while the Zamboni smooths the ice; and on this season-opening evening, every fan was given a rubber wristband with embedded LED lights that flashed in unison, controlled by an anonymous wizard behind a curtain somewhere in the arena. We were definitely not in Kansas anymore.

The fan experience was impressive. It is also impressive how the Predators' organization and the community have embraced P.K. Here is what Chris Junghans, the Predators' executive vice-president and chief revenue officer, said in an interview for this book about the game experience, the trade, and P.K.'s impact on the organization and the community.

CHRIS

THE GAME EXPERIENCE: We're not traditional, that's for sure. We play to the strengths of Music City. It's who we are and we are proud of it. Part of our spiel is, "Come here and you'll have a good time, regardless of what happens on the ice."

THE P.K. EXPERIENCE: We got our first taste of P.K. and got to know him during the All-Star Game [held on January 31, 2016]. P.K. was open to the city and he was out and about. He was enjoying the city and was seen at the concerts. A large part of Nashville got to see who P.K. was.

P.K. came here about three or four weeks after the trade with his mom, his two sisters, a marketing person out of Montreal, and a junior coach. In the very first meeting, we had no idea of the level of sophistication or professionalism he displayed. The first thing he says is, "Thank you for your time." This was a great sign [that] this is going to be wonderful working relationship. And the very next thing out of his mouth was, "I want to be clear. I am here to play hockey and win a Stanley Cup." And so, Sean Henry—my boss, the CEO—we sat back in our chairs and said, "Okay, we heard all we want to hear at this point." Now let's figure out how we can grow together and support one another.

He's just a smart athlete and he gets it. We are not even scratching the surface yet.

THE TRADE EXPERIENCE: The staff couldn't believe it. It was overwhelmingly positive. How did we get this bona fide superstar on our roster? There was jubilation over what we thought was the number one marquee player in the league and now he's playing in our gold jersey.

We worried publicly about trading [our captain] Shea Weber, a player we drafted and was the face of the franchise. I can tell you, we didn't hear one negative thing about the trade from season ticket holders, unlike the Canadiens [when P.K. was traded]. Our season ticket holders appreciated Shea's efforts, as we did, but they couldn't have been more excited to get P.K. here and have him play.

We had high expectations for this team given where we were last year [the 2015–16 season]. We got to Game 7 of the second round, the furthest we've ever gone. When we made the trade for P.K. the expectations were higher, both externally and internally. Given who we have and how long we have them, we feel we have a window here, not to win just one Stanley Cup, but compete for more and win multiple Cups. It's going to be exciting and that's our message here. This is just the beginning.

THE NASHVILLE EXPERIENCE: Nashville has never had a guy like P.K., in any sport. The professional sports franchises here are only twenty years old. The Tennessee Titans have never had a guy like P.K. The closest I think is [former quarterback] Steve McNair. He was a city hero. The city is ready for it and we think he is the perfect fit. Nashville is full of a lot of stars. [Predators centreman] Mike Fisher is married to the number one country music superstar in the world, Carrie Underwood. We kind of know how to deal with it.

No doubt, it was an exciting time in Nashville during P.K.'s first game, with the promise of many more to come. During the game, in which the Predators prevailed 3–2, text messages and emails from family and friends made my phone dance in my hand. Friends of P.K.'s in Montreal, nineteen of them, had gathered to watch the game and cheer for P.K. Taz texted me from Toronto to say she saw Maria and me on TV, dancing after P.K.'s goal.

After the game, in which P.K. was named the third star, we took the elevator down to the lounge where family can wait for the players. We wanted to say hi and goodbye to P.K., as the team was flying directly to Chicago to play the Blackhawks again the next night—a tough home-and-home series to open the season. After briefly seeing P.K. and some of his new teammates, we were also able to meet the Predators' general manager, David Poile, who had orchestrated the trade. He was gracious and charming to us and said how much he appreciated the gold dress pants P.K. wore that night before and after the game in honour of his new team.

Then Maria and I walked out onto the buzzing downtown Nashville streets. People and music flowed out of the honky-tonks as we made our way to our car. Every bar had a stage and a live band. It was a festival atmosphere featuring young, smiling faces, and some older smiling faces too. Music City. Smashville. Perhaps this dynamic, fun-loving city will also be known for hosting a Stanley Cup parade. It certainly felt like a possibility on that night.

Of course, I didn't dare to dream that just eight months after P.K.'s thrilling first game with the Predators, Nashville's diehard fans would come tantalizingly close to actually witnessing the spectacle of the Lord Stanley's Mug being paraded past the over-flowing bars and juke joints of Lower Broadway in Music City's downtown.

The Predators' season had its ups and downs, but the team managed to peak at just the right time, and they earned the eighth and final playoff spot in the Western Conference at the beginning

of April. When all sixteen teams in the Stanley Cup playoffs were
seeded by their regular season record, Nashville was sixteenth.

Being the last team to quality earned them the dubious privilege of playing the top-seeded team: the Chicago Blackhawks.
But the Predators were on fire, sweeping their rivals in four
games and sending a message to the rest of the league to watch
out. The team continued to climb the playoff ladder through
April and May, backstopped by the impressive goaltending of
Pekka Rinne. In the second round, the Predators took down
the St. Louis Blues in six games and then they went on to defeat
the Anaheim Ducks in six games, earning their first trip to the
Stanley Cup finals in the franchise's nineteen-year history. Their
rival would be the defending champions, Sidney Crosby and the
Pittsburgh Penguins.

It is hard to describe the intensity and emotion around seeing
your son play in the Stanley Cup finals. Once your team is in it,
then you are in it, for every minute of every game, until the final
buzzer sounds. I travelled to Nashville for most of the home
games with Maria, Natasha, Taz and the grandkids. Malcolm and
Jordan came to a number of games, when their schedules allowed.
The Predators organization was able to help us find hotels.

Many of my family and friends would not necessarily call
themselves hockey fans but are, more accurately, P.K. fans. The
more games the Predators played, and the more they won
during the playoffs, the more I was hearing from them. They
stayed up late to watch the action and were happy to connect
with me afterwards. Many would give me their play-by-play,
especially with matters connected to P.K. For them, he could

do no wrong, and their support made the experience even more special for Maria and me.

The Stanley Cup finals started in dramatic fashion for Team Subban. Maria, Natasha, Angelina and I drove to Pittsburgh on the day of Game 1. Delays at the border and driving with a thirteen-month-old made the trip a bit longer than we'd planned for. Street closures in the city meant we had to zigzag through the packed thoroughfares to the hotel. We were so close, yet so far away. We checked in quickly and rushed through the crowd of mostly Penguins fans in the lobby. We knew the drop of the puck in Game 1 of the Stanley Cup finals was imminent, but instead of being in our reserved seats, we were in a hotel waiting for an elevator.

When we got to our room I ditched our luggage and raced for the TV remote. My fingers commanded the buttons like a teenager texting. After a few taps, I found the game—and there was P.K. on the ice. Now it didn't matter where we were. The game was in front us. We watched as the puck moved into Pittsburgh's zone, then it found P.K.'s stick and quickly ended up in the back of the net—the first goal of the game.

"P.K. scored! Marieeeeee!" I screamed.

It didn't matter that we had just spent five-plus hours in a car. All my adrenaline set me off like a rocket and I was jumping and screaming with glee. I felt sorry for the people in the room below us.

Meanwhile, Taz and her twins, Honor and Epic, were already at the game, having flown in earlier that day. When P.K. scored, Taz was jumping high and screaming just like we were— but she and her boys were the only ones reacting with joy in her section of the PPG Paints Arena. She was marked a Predator fan for the rest of the evening as the spectators now took notice that the gold she was wearing was Nashville's hue and not Pittsburgh's.

Unfortunately, our excitement quickly turned to disbelief when the goal was challenged by the Pittsburgh coach, then overturned. Suddenly, Taz felt like a fish out of water. She told me later she wished that she could have disappeared into the fabric of her seat. Maria and I walked over to the arena and joined Taz before the end of the first period. Her husband, Andre, and their oldest son, Legacy, drove down that day and were also late, but eventually made it to the game, which was won by Pittsburgh, 5–3.

Once we are all together, it didn't take long for Penguins fans to realize who we were, a black family all wearing No. 76 Subban jerseys and T-shirts. The hometown fans couldn't wait to tell us how much they liked P.K. as a player, but they said they were impressed by his charitable work, particularly with the children's hospital. Strangers say these things to me all the time— and I never get tired of hearing them.

Two nights later, the Predators dropped the second game in the series. We were looking forward to getting to Nashville for the next two games and hopefully seeing things turn around.

The atmosphere in Nashville during playoff games is like nothing I have ever seen at any sporting event, including at any number of NHL games or at the Olympics in Sochi. Nashville is the most intense fan experience I have ever had. Inside the arena the noise is unbelievable, but you can also sense the immense crowds outside and around the city. For a town nicknamed

Music City, there was always a buzz surrounding which country music superstar would be belting out the national anthem that night. And you also came to expect seeing a catfish or two tossed out on the ice from the sea of gold jerseys and rally towels in the crowd—a good-luck tradition unique to Smashville. The many moments of fans displaying their incomparable team spirit fused together to make each game a fun and memorable event. It also helped that the Predators won Games 3 and 4 at home, to tie the series at two games apiece.

One of the luminaries in attendance at Game 4 was Hall of Fame basketball player Charles Barkley, in town during a break from his work as a television analyst during the NBA playoffs. He, too, was amazed with the celebratory atmosphere. After the game he made his way to the Predators' locker

Charles Barkley and Karl

room to meet P.K. Charles had recently seen P.K. featured on *E:60 Profile,* a popular program on ESPN. He told my son he wanted to meet me. The next thing I knew P.K. was telling me I had a dinner invitation from one of the greats of basketball, Sir Charles himself.

We met at a popular steak house later that evening. The restaurant was not crowded, but even if it had been I could have quickly picked that imposing figure out of a crowd. Charles gave me an enormous bear hug, enveloping me in his arms as if we were long-lost friends. Charles told me he was impressed with what I'd said on the *E:60 Profile* about how we should not let race, or anything else, distract us from reaching our goals or fulfilling our potential. Charles said he speaks to young people all the time and he gives them the same message I do. I knew of Charles Barkley as a basketball player, and then as a television personality, but now I became aware that he also sees himself as a teacher wanting to get the most out of his students.

Exchanging stories with Charles Barkley was a thrill that capped off an unforgettable night, but unfortunately for all Predators fans, Game 4 would be the last time we'd taste victory in the series. Pittsburgh won Game 5 at home and then triumphed in a nail-biter in Game 6 in Nashville, scoring with 1:35 left in the third period to break a scoreless tie. Seeing my son's name etched into the Stanley Cup was going to have to wait at least another year.

It took me a little time to process my feelings after having watched Sidney Crosby and his teammates hoist the Stanley

Cup in victory in front of 19,000 Predators' fans, none of whom were prepared for the season to end.

There are thirty teams in the NHL and each started the 2016–17 season with two main priorities: to win as many games as possible and to win the Stanley Cup. As it always goes, some teams will win more games than they lose and some will lose more games than they win, but only two teams will play for the cup in June. If you are playing hockey in June, you have had a successful season.

At the start of the playoffs, many hockey experts did not see Nashville playing hockey in June—but they forgot to tell the Predators' players and fans. The team triumphed over doubt, pushing themselves through injuries and persevering through setbacks. Perhaps most important, they were a united force to the last whistle. Even though P.K. and his teammates did not raise the Stanley Cup, the team succeeded in teaching everyone a lesson about what it takes to be a winner, on and off the ice.

As for me, upon arriving home in Nobleton I was pleased to receive a call with an offer I couldn't refuse: filling in for an absent principal at a Toronto school for a few weeks. I could not have found a better place to spend my time than in that environment after going through the roller coaster of emotions that accompanied the Predators' Stanley Cup run. It was good to be back around children running, playing, learning and smiling.

15

The Second Dream

I do not believe we are born to live just one dream. When I retired from the Toronto District School Board in 2013, I knew it was time to chase a second, long-held dream of mine—to become a public speaker. I felt compelled to share with as wide an audience as I could find what I have learned after thirty-five years of coaching, teaching and parenting, with a focus on developing potential in our children.

That June coincided with the Subban hat trick—when Jordan joined the Canucks organization, and all three brothers had now been drafted and signed to NHL teams. This milestone gave birth to the million-dollar question about the secret of our success: How did we do it?

Like a head chef creating a restaurant's signature meal, I have developed—over time, and by experimenting with different ingredients—the Team Subban Recipe for Success. This recipe now constitutes the substance of the speeches that make up my second career as a public speaker, and has been refined to three simple but effective ingredients: the three-legged stool, the four Ts and life's drive-thru.

The Three-Legged Stool

The three-legged stool is one of the earliest forms of furniture. It consists of a seat and three legs. In the Subban Recipe for Success, the seat represents potential, and the three legs are the elements that work together to support the seat. If the legs aren't working together, that stool will not stand on its own, let alone support a person. To make our potential work for us, we must put its legs to good use. Each leg equally supports the growth of our potential. One leg is the dream, or big goal, that your potential calls for in order to develop. The second leg is the fortified belief system that will protect potential from the doubts and the doubters that will appear along the journey. The third leg represents the action we must take to reach our potential. Dreaming and believing, without taking action, are like a stool with only two legs. We are not born preachers, teachers, writers, doctors, gardeners or authors. Our potential gives us the ability, capacity, skills and talent to become those things.

Dream

P.K., Malcolm and Jordan's ascent in the hockey ranks started with an interest in the sport that developed into a dream. Today, P.K. is at the top of hockey's pyramid, and Malcolm and Jordan are close to the top. As young players develop, a pruning takes place, reducing the number of players. Some lose motivation. Some develop other interests. Some just stop dreaming. And there are some who give up on playing. It was a love for the game and a drive to be better that kept my boys moving up.

Belief System

While chasing dreams, you will battle doubters and your own doubts. That is why you need the second leg of the stool. You need to believe in your potential, in your abilities and in your dream. How do you fortify your belief system? By feeding it with the following words: "My potential lies inside me. It gives me the ability to reach for something, to become something better." These words play over and over in my mind. When doubts appear, they are quickly wiped out. Forces of distraction—whether internal or external—are our most formidable opponents. You need both a strong mind and body to fulfill your potential.

Action

A lot of people get stuck when it comes to taking action. They allow their minds to stop them before they start. The great British artist, architect, poet, critic and social thinker John Ruskin insightfully said, "What we think or what we know or what we believe, is in the end, of little consequence. The only consequence is what we do." Without action, potential resembles an iceberg. You are only operating at the tip of your potential. The largest piece is below the surface or hidden away deep inside you.

The Four Ts

When I reflect on our boys' hockey achievement, I am able to group their engagement into four categories. I call them the four Ts: time, task, training and team.

First, you must invest *time* if you want to become better, and the earlier you start the better off you will be. P.K., Malcolm and Jordan made time and used time to focus on the second category: their hockey *tasks*. This included things such as skating, shooting pucks, stickhandling, playing shinny, playing mini sticks in the hallway and watching hockey games on television, or Don Cherry's hockey videos.

The third T is *training*. I have learned that it takes many attempts to grow your talent and to find your God-given ability. The essence of training is found in what I call being "married to practice": living with it and dreaming about getting better every day. Taking ten skating or shooting lessons is not being married to practice—it's more like going on a date. You are not serious about the relationship. We do not get better overnight. We get better over time. Anders Ericsson and Robert Pool have researched and written about the thousands of hours it takes to develop expertise. It's also important to remember that the way you train is vital to success. You don't develop expertise by constantly working in your skill range or comfort zone. You must push yourself and take chances.

The fourth T is *team*. The bigger the dream, the more important the team. Our children need a team they believe in, and one that believes in them too. Children must be taught how to be a good teammate; it's a learned skill. When P.K. was packing his bags for Belleville and getting ready to leave home at sixteen, I remember telling him he would have to work to get his teammates to like him. He didn't fully comprehend what I meant then, but I am sure he knows now.

Life's Drive-Thru

The drive-thru is ubiquitous in our society. I believe our lives present us with a series of drive-thrus. My sons and my daughters are going through them. I am going through them. Companies and corporations are going through them too.

As you approach a drive-thru to get your coffee or food, you are likely to encounter a "Do Not Enter" sign. If you ignore the sign, you risk getting into an accident and will not reach your destination and get what you came to buy. Entering the wrong way is a distraction from your goal—and life has many distractions. The minute you take them on they become your goal and give birth to excuses for not achieving what you set out to do.

If you've followed the "Enter Here" directions, the first station in the drive-thru is the order window. This is where we place our order in the form of dreams or goals. What do we want out of life? What do we want out of our relationships? Who do we want to be? What do *you* want to do? It's time to place your order.

The final stage is the pick-up window, where you pay the price before you get what you ordered. Only those who pay the price get what they want in life; you pay for what you get—and you get what you pay for.

I have found these stories, these lessons, resonate with audiences. It doesn't matter which group I have been invited to speak to—students, parents, coaches, educators, business owners, community agencies, farmers, financial advisors or insurance officials—everyone appreciates some inspiration and direction. While I will tailor aspects of my speeches to each audience, my main purpose in talking to them is to touch hearts and stimulate minds. One time, after I had made an emotional speech to the entire student body and staff at Brookview Middle School, teacher Darlene Jones told me I should have been a preacher. While that's a road I did not take, I certainly feel I'm in my element in front of large groups of people.

When I give speeches, I use a lapel microphone, and I am always on the move. The most powerful thing for me is when I am close enough to someone to look in their eyes. If there are five hundred people, I want to see a thousand eyes before my hour is up. I never have enough time to say all I want to say, so the question-and-answer sessions that follow each presentation give me another chance to connect with people, which can be extremely rewarding.

It is December 2016 and my hockey-playing sons are coming home just days before Christmas. For Maria and me, the boys being at home is one gift that is not wrapped in a box. Since 2005, when P.K. was drafted by the Belleville Bulls and, in subsequent years, when Malcolm and Jordan followed in his footsteps, Christmas has been the time to close the gap between our sons' hockey dreams and our home. With the girls working and the boys playing hockey it can be difficult for us to get together during the hockey season, which is one reason why the Christmas season is so special.

As the boys grew older, the hockey distance between them and home grew exponentially. Maria and I travel to see them, but I realize, too, that it is important not to crowd them. They need their space to grow up without us holding their hands or tying their skates. The same space that was working for them was working to make our hearts heavy at times, especially when the roller coaster of their careers has taken them to a low point. Sometimes I find myself complaining, mostly to myself, about not having them around more often. On the one hand, I am happy for them; on the other, I am saddened by the distance that separates us, even though I can watch them on television almost nightly or speak to them almost daily, often at any given minute. A family that talks together gets together and stays together.

This year, we didn't get to stay together long. Malcolm had to leave on Christmas Day to return to Providence; Jordan and P.K. were able to stay only until Boxing Day before returning to their teammates in Utica and Nashville. So our big get-together was planned for December 24.

Our home felt happy, welcoming and dressed-up for the season, with poinsettias perched on wooden stands, festive tablecloths covering the dining tables and reggae Christmas music spilling from ceiling speakers. In the corner of the room stood our large Christmas tree, and underneath it the many gifts we would open the next morning after breakfast. There was a gift for everyone. But the most important gifts this holiday season were not found under our tree but in the presence of the ones we love.

Maria and I were up with the roosters on Christmas Eve morning, working on creating the tantalizing smells of ham, turkey, curry goat, oxtail and seafood that filled the house. Taz contributed her traditional squash soup to the feast, and Tasha made macaroni pie and banana cake. Our hungry crowd was already salivating, but there were still hours to go before our sit-down dinner late that afternoon.

Maria and I have been preparing Christmas dinners for years and have never been able to serve them at the scheduled time. And while dinner is not on time, hunger is never late. We told everyone not to eat a lot because we would be eating early, but every time someone walked by the kitchen island, a piece of white icing was taken off Aunty Joy's Christmas cake. As time passed, hunger started to speak. "What are you guys doing? You said that we would be eating early," someone complained from the family room adjacent to the kitchen. The sounds and voices coming from a movie playing on the TV and the grandchildren running, jumping and screaming made it difficult to hear. I guess this is what family love sounds like. I think I like it.

It was finally time to eat; the dining room table was set, and the food laid out on the kitchen island. I motioned to P.K. to turn the TV off and then called everyone to stand around the island. It wasn't long before everyone was gathered and attentive, including the little ones. Our usual routine is that one person says grace, and then Mom and Dad say, "Let's eat." I changed things this year. Before the grace, I thanked Maria for preparing a magnificent spread for the family. I thanked her for taking care of us. I knew she was tired, but she always finds a way to persevere.

Then I asked each family member to think of one word to share to describe what it meant to be home together for Christmas—a one-word prayer. Initially there was silence; then Malcolm and P.K. both volunteered to start the ball rolling. Malcolm went first, offering the word *grateful*. One by one the words were called out: *healthy, happy, eat, cake, blessed, thankful, love, honour, appreciative*. My word was *you*. I pointed to each person present and said, "You and you and you matter. You are important to us. That is why we do all that we do. Mom and Dad did it all for you."

Finally, our grandson Legacy delivered the grace, sung from his young heart to the tune of "Frère Jacques":

> Thank you, Jesus, thank you, Jesus,
> For our food, for our food.
> Many, many blessings,
> Many, many blessings.
> Amen, Amen.

Another gift of the season was Angelina Christina Maria Subban Gaynor, our first granddaughter, born in April. This was the first Christmas for the latest addition to Team Subban. She is the daughter of Tasha and her fiancé, Tamar Gaynor. Angelina is a happy baby, and that happiness is contagious. She greets you with a smile along with outstretched arms ready to conquer you. The boys will FaceTime almost daily to see Angelina, along with grandsons Legacy, Epic and Honor. Our four grandchildren also give us a special gift each year by allowing us to experience the magic of the season through their innocent eyes.

I look at our five children and can't help but feel pride. Where my children have placed their minds, their feet have followed. The boys are chasing their professional hockey dreams. P.K. is living his dream, while Malcolm and Jordan are still chasing theirs. Taz and Tasha are working as educators with the Toronto District School Board, helping young minds give birth to dreams that they, too, will chase. Taz has a master's degree in education and is a high-school teacher; Tasha, who has a teaching and fine arts degree, teaches in an elementary school. They love their profession and working with children. (If you are a teacher and don't love children, your days will be long and your nights sleepless.) The girls are independent and ambitious and, like the boys, understand that making meaningful change is a slow process that happens over time.

Maria and I did not start out with a master plan for raising our children; however, nothing we did was accidental. My five children were the guinea pigs for a system. You see, child rearing is also a long process, the goal of which is the growth of potential. Parenting is about our children getting better, and parents getting better too. If you are not thinking about getting better as a parent, it makes it difficult for your kids to do the same.

The growing and learning never stops. That goes for me and Maria and our five children. We have four grandchildren who are all learning and growing. There are dreams all around them, like flowers in a garden. My grandsons are learning to skate in the shadow of their uncles. My five children are all doing something they love to do, and they are committed to doing and being their best.

It is easy to get lost in life's process maze. I worked in a school that was not achieving based on a number of metrics. Doing better was the missing link with students, staff and parents. The mentality was to fix these children. But they were not broken. The mindset had to change; it had to be about how to make them want to be better.

It often takes time to see the results of the efforts we as educators pour into children, to know you made a lasting connection to an eleven-year-old that will pay off when he or she is in high school, or even years later. I recently received an email that nearly had me crying. It was from Taz's husband, Andre Bobb, who teaches in Toronto at a high school that includes a fair number of Brookview Middle School graduates. Andre sent me a writing assignment from one of his students that he knew would be of great interest to me. He was right. The writing assignment was from Jennifer Tran:

Where I'm From

I am from bright blue skies,
with a touch of sunshine.
Running around, blowing bubbles
in my grandma's colourful garden.
Raspberries, lettuce, tomatoes
and so much more,
will soon turn into a dinner

for a giant family get-together.
From loads of fights to crazy talks,
that ends with loud laughs and memories.
Endless memories,
that will always be with me.

I am from the bulging eyes of strangers,
glaring at me and someone I call
my beloved twin sister.
I am from baking cookies for Santa
on Christmas Eve.
Cookie cutters, and flour everywhere,
"Oh, no! What a mess we've made!"
but no worries,
Mamabear is always there to save the day.

I am from summer air
that has a hint of weed,
followed by the sounds of shots being fired.
During the months of May and July,
I tell myself the noises I hear outside
are just fireworks,
but somewhere inside,
I know an innocent man is about to die.
I am from a little house.
A house built for four,
but I live with twelve,
and that's three times more.
I am from Tuesday night tacos,
Five siblings, five tacos,

each one of a kind,
happily ending with no fights.

I am from the words of Mr. Karl Subban,
A principal who taught me
that practice and hard work
doesn't make us perfect,
it makes us better.
Not only the things we do,
it also allows us to become better people.
Words that have been implanted in my mind,
that I'll treasure forever.

I am from big bright smiles,
that show I'm fine,
but inside is a strong wall.
Built from pain, dark secrets and shame.
Created by the ones
who are supposed to love.
Sooner or later this wall will fall.
I will be knocked down,
but I will not be knocked out.
I am from the moments
that keep me standing here.
This is me.
I'm sorry.

Thank you, Jennifer, for this beautiful gift. With a combi-
nation of grace, joy, innocence and heartache, Jennifer has
created a powerful message. This is what it is like for so many

students growing up in the Jane-Finch neighbourhood of Toronto. Having Andre share Jennifer's assignment with me reminded me again of Henry Adams's words: "A teacher affects eternity; he can never tell where his influence stops."

In February 2017, Maria and I were back in Grenada visiting our friends Sally and Ron for a few weeks. While on the island, we toured a local attraction, a spice factory. As we entered the compound, I said hello to the security guard and asked how he was doing. He returned the greeting and then asked, "Where are you from?" I wasn't thinking too deeply about this routine question, so I was somewhat surprised by my own answer. "Sometimes I forget where I am from," I told the guard earnestly. "That is why I only worry about where I am going."

Where do you want to go? What is your dream? Whatever it is you want to do or be, I hope you have taken from this book that you must make time to do it, practise it, train for it and work with others while others work with you. That is how you grow potential. It is only when you reach for something that you learn what you are truly capable of achieving. This book cannot tie your skates for you and drive you to practice at 6 a.m., but my hope is that it will guide you and motivate you to find what you love to do in life, to continue striving to be better and to pass that message on to the children in your life. And I will be in the stands, cheering for you.

EPILOGUE:

Growing Up Subban

Who better to describe what it was like growing up in the Subban family than our five kids? Maria and I did our best to provide for our children and give them opportunities to succeed; to be firm but fair; to guide them and inspire them while also disciplining them. It wasn't easy and it wasn't always pretty, but I can say that we were always there for our children, and they grew up knowing we cared. (Taz and Tasha were interviewed together in the dining room of our former family home in Rexdale, where Taz is now raising her three sons with her husband, Andre; P.K., Malcolm, and Jordan were interviewed separately.)

THE KIDS SPEAK
Siblings

Tasha: Growing up, P.K. and I probably spent the most
          time together, besides Malcolm and Jordan. We
          went up to our grandparents' in Sudbury every
          summer until my grandmother passed away in
          2000. P.K. and I would stay the entire summer.
          That means I got to do back-to-school shopping
          without everybody else around. All summer I would
          go through the Walmart flyers, circling all of the
          things I wanted.

          Every summer it was our thing to go blueberry
          picking. My grandparents would say, "Do not eat
          the blueberries when you are out in the forest." Of
          course, we never listened. P.K. is shoving them in
          his mouth. I'm shoving them in my mouth. Of
          course, we get diarrhea two hours later, right?

          The thing with P.K. and me is, we always
          fought. We used to get it on. I mean, to the point
          where we gave my dad mini heart attacks.

          We'd fight over the TV because we only had
          one. He would be sitting down watching his stupid
          Rock'em Sock'em Don Cherry videos. The only
          things I ever liked to watch were *Family Matters*,
          Fresh Prince, and *The Young and the Restless*. What
          boy wants to watch *The Young and the Restless*?

Taz: And *Sailor Moon*.

Tasha: And *Sailor Moon*. So P.K. would come and take
          the converter and hide it and run. He'd put it
          somewhere else in the house. My dad is screaming,
          "Where is the converter?" My mom would be

saying, "What are you guys fighting about?" Then
he'd take his videotapes and put them in front of—

Taz: The sensor.

Tasha: —of the sensor, so I couldn't turn the channel if I
            had the converter. My dad used to get so mad at us
            because we would just duke it out. At that point I
            was stronger because I'm older. Then, slowly, as we
            got older, it became a bit of a game. If I was sleep-
            ing, he'd be pinching me.

Taz: You used to pinch each other under the arm and
            run away, and you couldn't pinch the other person
            back for twenty minutes.

Tasha: To this day, we still do it. P.K. comes home and he
            says, "Get away from me." I don't even know who
            came up with this stupid game. Now P.K. and I are
            older and running his business. We're doing every-
            thing together and it's weird. Mom said, "I would
            never, ever see you two join forces to do some-
            thing together." But, at the end of the day, he's my
            brother. I'm his sister. If anybody talks about P.K.,
            I'll rip their head off. If anybody talks about me,
            he'll protect me.

Taz: We always played together and didn't really play
            outside with the other kids. We used to record our-
            selves. That was a big thing. I would record myself
            doing news reports or singing or playing the piano.
            Mom has all the videos.

Malcolm: Sometimes we used the piano as the net for mini
            sticks. They told us not to do that. We used to
            watch wrestling, *SmackDown* and *Raw*, and copy
            the moves on the bed with the pillows. The bed
            would be smashed. We used pillows; we wouldn't do

the moves on each other. Actually, the only move we would do on each other was the figure-four leg-lock. We did that all the time. Ric Flair. You couldn't do those other moves without hurting someone.

Tasha, P.K., Taz

Girls and Hockey

Taz: I would not [have wanted] to play hockey. No, no.
            I stopped skating by twelve. My last memory of
            skating was being in the change room and getting
            hot chocolate, trying to warm my feet. I'd wear
            double socks and nothing worked. I get that you
            need to start kids on something from an early age.
            I think about [my son] Legacy. Legacy doesn't know
            anything but skating. He just thinks that is some-
            thing you do. He assumes everyone can skate. For
            us, it was the girls play basketball and the boys play
            hockey and that's the way it goes.

Tasha: I wouldn't want to play hockey, but I was fascinated
            with figure skaters. I used to try to emulate them
            on the ice. I was a pretty good skater. I would do
            my crossovers and try to do a little bit of spinning
            and go on one leg. Usually when P.K. was skating,
            I would go with them—except to Nathan Phillips
            Square till two in the morning. I enjoyed playing
            basketball but it wasn't like how Taz enjoyed it. I'm
            more of—I would say I was the lazier one out of
            everybody. I'm just going to admit it.

Strict Rules

Taz: There were no sleepovers. We were not going to
            hang out at somebody's house.

Tasha: Also, "You're not walking in the mall on a Saturday
            afternoon."

Taz: No.

Tasha: Mom would say, "Go find something constructive to do." Dad would say, "You know what, Maria? Get them a book. Let's find a book." And you'd have to read it.

Even now my brothers will be out [in Toronto at night], and we live far in Nobleton, and they always come home. P.K. has tons of money—he can do whatever he wants—but he always comes home.

We never, ever slept out. Not even at cousins' houses. We were told: "You come home. If you guys are going to go out and have fun, you bring your ass home. We want you to be there in the morning."

It's funny. Now with us being older—I'm twenty-nine—if I want to go out with my friends, it's the same thing. I always make sure I leave where I'm going so I have enough time to get home.

Taz: With a Caribbean upbringing, you stay with your family. You do what you are supposed to do. There are no sleepovers. Because that's when issues happen. Some people would say, "Oh, you guys need to have fun." We actually did. Yeah, our parents were strict, but they were strict for a reason. And in retrospect, I'm—

Tasha: Now I'm glad.

Taz: I'm glad they were that strict because now I get it.

Kids' Choice

Tasha: High school was my rebellious time. I ended up quitting basketball. I focused on being an artist. It was funny, because most people, the way my parents were, they ask, "If P.K. wanted to quit hockey, would they have let him?" And I say, of course. They would have said, "Are you sure?" Like my mom said to him when he was a certain age, "Before I start shovelling all this money, is this what you want to do? I can put my money somewhere else and we can be driving lavish cars and stuff."

Taz: Taking a vacation.

Tasha: Exactly. They never, ever pressured us by saying, "You need to be playing this sport and doing this in school." It was, "You need to have your priorities straight": school, a sport, some type of extracurricular activity, and family. We had that choice, where I think a lot of people don't understand that. They think when they hear the story of P.K. going skating all the time, training all these times, that it was like our parents forced it on him. Absolutely not.

Taz: They introduced it to us. Then, at a certain age, you had a choice whether or not you wanted to continue. I feel, with kids, when you find something you are good at, you want to continue. If you are not introduced to it, you don't develop a skill for it, a knack for it; then it becomes frustrating. I feel because they introduced us to it, we liked it. I liked basketball. We got to travel; I got to play on different teams; I got to meet different people.

           I have a student right now at Westview Centennial, and I said to her, "You are involved in everything. Why?" She said, "I get out of the house." Because her parents are strict, like how my parents were. But they're constructive outings, which I think is more beneficial in the long run, right?

Tasha: With me being rebellious in high school, there
              were times I didn't take my education as seriously—
              I went from being way up high in math to having
              to go to summer school. My parents laid it down.
              "Listen, this is what is going to happen. You are
              not going to go to school dances. If we don't see
              an improvement in this, we are not going to
              give you this reward." I even remember missing
              a few tournaments in basketball. My parents
              got me a tutor. Then I started to pick it up . . .
              I started to realize, looking at everyone around
              me, that I needed to get my socks up. When
              I graduated I ended up getting a scholarship
              from my high school.

              No Excuses

Tasha: My dad never made excuses for us. I remember
              in high school, a teacher said to me, and she shall
              remain nameless, she said—this was in grade twelve,
              when I started to pick up everything, my marks
              were getting good—"What do you want to do?"
              I said, "I want to be a doctor." She said, "You can't
              be a doctor. Are you sure you don't want to be a
              nurse's assistant?" She said that to me in the library.
              I came home and told my dad, and he said, "You
              can't be a doctor. Look at your math marks." And
              he was right. My mom said, "Karl, you don't say
              that! You can't say that!" In retrospect, yes, you
              don't say that to a student. And I would never take
              that approach, but that was my dad's way of tough
              love: "I'm going to tell you, but you should be

embarrassed that somebody else said that to you and I'm telling you the same thing." When this happened, I picked everything up. I got early acceptance to university and that was motivation for me.

Now a lot of parents would go in and yell at the teacher, go to the principal and justify the child's behaviour. I could have crumbled and stared crying, but I said, "You know what? I am going to show that woman that I'm going to be something and I'm going to be something great. I didn't become a doctor but everything is good-to-go now. Dad never made excuses for us. It didn't matter what it was. Even till this day, he does not make excuses for us. He will always challenge us.

If somebody called us the N-word and we went home and said it, my dad would turn around and say, "Who cares? Is that going to stop you from doing this? Is this going to stop you from doing that?" Mom would be the more reasoning one. "Oh, you know what, Karl? People can't be saying those things. But you know what? To hell with them." That is one thing I try to emulate as a teacher with students. When people try to put you down, which we've all dealt with, you can't let that affect you, because if you are so concerned with that you are never going to get anywhere. And that is the thing both my mom and dad tried to push. Think of all the things people say about P.K. If he really sat there and embraced it, he would not be playing hockey today, especially at the level he is playing. As a new parent, I would definitely be the same way.

Taz: Yep, same here. I tell my students all the time that
            excuses are for losers. You gotta get it done.
            No excuses.

Tasha: Then it becomes a big argument. Even with P.K.,
            just two weeks ago, when he was going through that
            whole thing of giving over the puck in the last few
            minutes of the game, my dad would tell him, "Just
            get the puck, make a move, move on! I don't want
            to hear anything about your skates. I don't want to
            hear about your edges not being sharpened, that
            they are not good. I don't want to hear that!"

            P.K. is like, "Dad!"

            "Well, P.K., just make a move and that's it. Just
            move the puck!"

Taz: I feel, when you are in professional sports, every-
            one is like, "You're amazing. You're the best thing
            since sliced bread." But P.K. calls home, and he calls
            dad basically every day, because he still needs that
            grounding. Dad's going to give it to him and give it
            to him straight, right?

Tasha: Dad was saying, "Why does he keep doing that? He
            doesn't need to do that!" We are all just sitting there,
            quiet. I remember that night. He went upstairs to his
            room. "I'm going to go write my book." He closed
            the door, and it was dark [in there]. We're like, "Dad,
            you're not writing your book in the dark."

Taz: He gives you stuff to talk about.

Tasha: Always. Always. He leaves us the choice, and I
            think that's a good thing. Dad always raised us up
            to be critical thinkers, to have that mindset. He
            always says, "If A doesn't work, are B and C and D
            options? What do I have to do next?"

Malcolm: He instilled in us the idea that no one cares about
            your excuses. If you want it, you have to go get it;
            you have to prove to everyone you want it, that you
            deserve it. There are no days off. He stood behind
            his words, so that helped us a lot.

P.K.:   I give him full marks, but I got to tell you, a lot of
            parenting is on the child. All they can do is give you
            all the tools and discipline you the best way that
            they can, but once you step out in the real world
            you have your own decisions to make. When I look
            at my parents, they did exactly what they were sup-
            posed to do, which was to give you the tools to be
            successful in life. At the end of the day, when they
            give you those tools, it's your choice if you want to
            use them and how to use them.

            You talk about different things, social things
            that we go through as kids, whether you're going to
            school and you have friends who are doing drugs
            and drinking alcohol. The choices you make there
            are so important. But I always say to kids, "Making
            a wrong decision does not mean your life is over.
            What is your goal in life?" Your family and your
            parents can help you mould that, but it's up to you
            to execute it.

            My dad doesn't go and work out in the gym for
            me every day; he doesn't go and get treatment for me
            every day; he doesn't eat healthy food for me every
            day; he doesn't sleep ten hours a night for me. I
            have to be disciplined to do those things. So parent-
            ing only goes so far. Ultimately, it comes down to,
            "Okay, how bad do I want this? How bad do I want
            to be successful in life?"

No Furniture

Taz:	We had no furniture.
Tasha:	We had, like, a couch.
Taz:	My boyfriend at the time, now my husband, he and his friend came over and said, "Oh, are you guys moving?"
Tasha:	You know what happened to us? We destroyed the furniture as kids.
Taz:	So my mom said, "We're not buying anything else."
Tasha:	We were destructive. People in my family would say, "Oh, Karl and Maria, your kids are destroying the house." My mom would say, "I work hard for my damn house. If my kids want to destroy it, you leave them alone. We'll deal with it."
	Who cares, right? The house is still here. All the walls, everything is still up. Caribbean people, I think, are very materialistic.
Taz:	It's about everything looking pristine. Some people live like that, but when you have kids, everything can't be perfect. It just can't be, because then the kids don't want to play. They're going to just sit there and stare at the walls?
	There would be puck marks on the walls—and the mini sticks. Mom used to start hiding them.
Tasha:	I did too. I used to watch *Young and the Restless*, and Jordan would get these freaking mini sticks and be playing right here [in the hallway]. It was just so annoying, and you would hear him, I mean, a full three hours. So I would take the sticks and hide them. When we moved, he said, "There's all

my effin' mini sticks." There were, like, twenty-five, thirty, under my mattress.

Jordan: Tasha used to hide my mini sticks because I was up so early in the morning banging away. I remember my favourite time of the day used to be when everyone was gone so I could just play by myself and have no one walking through and interrupting my game. I scored, like, I don't know, ten thousand, fifty thousand goals in my mini-sticks career. It was all imagination, man. I just loved playing so much that I never got sick of it. I just imagined different things every time I played. I played Game 7 in the Stanley Cup Finals every day in my hallway. Always scored the winning goal. The overtime goal. Every day.

Sacrifices

Taz: Grad trips, school functions, we never missed any of those. They found a way to get it done, to get it paid. They didn't show us behind the scenes. Something had to get cut. Mom didn't have her hair done every week; she didn't have her nails done every week. She wasn't going to the spa.

Tasha: I remember my basketball coach, the year before I quit, he said, "When are your parents going to get me that money?" It was $1,500. My mom said, "She'll have it for you." Mom wrote a cheque. It was postdated for another six weeks. When he sees me now he says, "Your parents, they sacrificed a lot."

Taz: They didn't expect anything for free.

Tasha: They would say, "I can only pay this much, so if I have to give you fifty dollars a month for my daughter to play, that's what we are going to do, based on the fact I have five kids."

Malcolm: My mom stopped working to stay home and look after us. My dad pretty much had no time to himself because of all the time he spent driving us to school and to hockey and doing stuff when we weren't in school or at hockey, like the backyard rink, taking us to the community rink, shooting pucks in the driveway—it was crazy. Definitely a lot of time he put into us, and it's definitely paying off now. So we can't thank him enough, obviously. And my mom staying home, getting us ready for school and doing all the little things, and making our food and making sure we were eating healthy and packing our lunch, helping us with homework. It's actually unbelievable how much time they put into us.

Jordan: I think people see the rewards, but behind the scenes, there's a lot of things, you know, blood, sweat, and tears, that were put into this. Without that, none of us would be where we are today.

Discipline

Tasha: Let's put it this way: I heard my dad saying it—and it's funny, because I say it to my students—"Do not embarrass us. Do not embarrass me and my name—our name." That was our thing.

Discipline was cleaning or chores. TV was gone. Mom would roll up the PlayStation. And there was

Jordan and Malcolm

yelling—Dad was a yeller—but not grounding. You're not going to miss practice. Because it's not about you. It's about the team.

I remember when I was nineteen I wanted to go out to a club with my friends. I had my G2, but we only had one car, so I couldn't take the car. You know what my parents did? They drove me to the club and they picked me back up at 4 a.m. My friends would say, "Your parents are unbelievable."

At first you'd feel embarrassed, but then I didn't care. Then my friends would say, "Can your parents drop us off at home? My parents would say, "Sure, we'll drop all of you girls home." And I think we are going to be the exact same way [with our kids].

Taz: Yeah, I'm going to be.

Jordan: My parents were no-nonsense people. I remember one time I was going to the Big Nickel Tournament in Sudbury. I got a bad grade on one of my tests, and my mom wouldn't let me. My dad had to convince her to let me go. The only reason I was allowed to go was because I was allowed to do a retest and I got a good grade.

Younger Brothers

Tasha: Malcolm and Jordan are growing up differently. My dad, we had a big argument about this recently.

Taz: We had way more rules. These guys are driving cars—

Tasha: They have their own cars at sixteen.

Taz: I'm like, what? We were taking the bus.

Tasha: Malcolm and Jordan. They wouldn't know. Like P.K. always says to them, "When I first started training, I used to take the bus downtown, come back, go to sleep, go back down, come back home and sleep. I never had a car to drive." My dad will stick up for Malcolm and Jordan. "Oh no, they work just as hard."

Taz: They have no clue.

Tasha: They have no clue, because they're just in a different era. Right?

Taz: Now P.K. is sounding like the old man. "Oh yeah, you guys should be doing this, this, and that." And he sounds like my dad.

Tasha: Exactly. He says everything just like my dad. We say P.K. is going to be exactly like my dad when he has kids. Exactly like him.

Malcolm the Goalie

Tasha: Malcolm is always in his goalie equipment. That's one thing he used to do. At night, this guy's a psycho. He would come in here and put on—he still does it at home; he was just doing it in the garage the other day—he puts on his full goalie equipment—

Taz: And just hang out.

Tasha: And hang out and play in-between the posts. Dead serious. Pads, everything—downstairs, doing his whole thing, movements, everything. Just on his own. Nobody's telling him. And my dad would be like, "What the hell? Where's Malcolm?" And all you hear in the basement is the equipment going "whoosh."

Famous Brother

Taz: I was working at George Harvey [Collegiate Institute] when P.K. had just made the World Junior team, and a girl at my school, her brother was a huge hockey fan, and she said, "Your brother is P.K. Subban? How come you never said anything?"
          I said, "I don't know. I guess he just plays hockey."
          She says, "Oh my God, I can't believe you didn't tell

anybody." I didn't know what to say. Now at school, everybody pretty much knows. You have to deal with stuff, like, "Why are you still working? Your brother is in the NHL."

Tasha: All the time. Teachers say the same thing.

Taz: I say, "If he gave all his millions away, he wouldn't have millions. I'm not his wife, guys, I'm his sister."

Now if there is something in the news, I hear, "Oh my God, is your brother going to be okay? Did you hear what happened?" They'll come to me and tell me something and I don't have cable TV so we don't always hear everything right away. Then I have to go read up on it.

But it can be cool . . . I remember one time I was at a store and a kid had a No. 76 jersey. I asked him why and he said, "Because P.K. Subban is my favourite player."

I said, "I'm his sister."

"Oh my God, you're his sister!" That is cute, when you see a kid—

Tasha: She's keen for doing that.

Taz: When you see the kids react, it's too cute.

Tasha: I don't say anything. I don't want anyone to ask me anything. My brothers, even though they are in the public eye, it's still private. A lot of my friends have said to me, "You guys are really one of the most down-to-earth sets of people, because you haven't changed."

Taz: We're not walking around with fur coats.

Tasha: Even now, as a teacher, it's hard. I remember when P.K. was swearing. He did that interview with

Sportsnet and he was angry. I was surprised because he usually keeps his composure. I thought, "Oh, you idiot. Now I have to go to school tomorrow and all these kids are going to be asking, 'Why's he swearing on TV?'"

That's where it interferes with teaching. The students want to veer off, and then they get you into it and you're talking, like, forty-five minutes about your life, and I have to say, "No, guys, we've got to get back to math."

Taz:　　They are very intrigued; I will say that. People will introduce me as P.K. Subban's sister, but once they get to know you they figure, "She's doing her own thing." . . . I think they expect you to be all snooty and, "Oh, I'm P.K. Subban's sister." Listen, it's here today, gone tomorrow.

Tasha:　　Yeah, anything can happen. That's why P.K. says, "I'm going to suck up all this time I have right now because it's not going to last forever." It's not. And we tell people that all the time. And when they ask, "Oh, does he come and show off with you?" I'm like, "No, because I'll put his ass right on the ground." You know what I mean?

Taz:　　I feel that piece of family keeps him grounded. Every time you think, "Okay, I'm better than the world," you get back to reality very quickly. And that's another reason he visits the hospital quite a bit. He was doing that before, even before he gave any money.

Middle Child

P.K.:   There's always a lot of chatting about the middle child in every family, that we have it the toughest—you don't know if you're young or if you're old, or if the expectations of you are to be mature or, you know, you're still growing up.

It's always hard to find your groove, but for me it was a little different. Hockey was a big part of my life growing up, and I think everybody in our family, including the kids, knew how badly I wanted to play in the NHL and how hard I worked. I think once that happened, even though I was a middle child, I felt that in some sort of way I was becoming more of a leader in the family and somebody to be relied upon to do all the right things and be mature and act mature. As I got older, even though maybe I was only fifteen or sixteen, playing semi-professional hockey—being the first one to go through it, and everybody seeing you go through changes in your life—came with expectations.

So I think it was always tougher for me. Even when I was growing up and I'd make stupid mistakes, it was always like the expectations were for me not to make those mistakes, whereas for my brothers, they were always younger, so it was, "Oh, he's still growing up." But for me it was, "No, the expectations are for you to know better than that." But I loved that, and that is probably why I'm so comfortable being in the position I'm in now as a professional athlete. Everything's under a microscope and magnified—and that's really when I operate my best.

Being a Role Model

P.K.:   It's the work ethic that you put in, right? So for me,
               I think developing that work ethic rubbed off on
               my family members a lot—my brothers, my sisters.
               And for them, they saw nothing was ever given to
               me, nothing came easy. I worked for everything
               I've received. So now I kind of get a little bit more
               leeway and a little bit more of a cushion because
               I put the work in, and they obviously know what
               I'm trying to accomplish.

               I'd say it starts with the person. I had a great
               support team around me when I was growing up,
               but ultimately it came down to . . . [hockey] was
               my passion—that's what I wanted. So the pressure
               was more internal, I would say, than external.

               Some of the things are trial and error, and I can
               only coach [my brothers] so much. Some of the
               things they're going to have to go and figure out
               themselves; for instance, going into a new team,
               or profession, or getting to another level in your
               profession. You have to feel it out and find out how
               you need to be to move forward, how to progress.

Dad as Coach and Principal

Malcolm: I think he was harder on me. The toughest thing
               for a coach is to understand your players. Who
               maybe needs to be pushed, who needs to be left
               alone more. Knowing how much potential one of
               your players has—can you get it out of him or not?
               My dad will understand me better than any other

player, so in that sense, he'll know when to push
and how much to push me.

Jordan: When he was my principal he was always extra hard
on me because he didn't want anyone to think that
I was getting special treatment. But it wasn't very
hard for him because I was always getting into
trouble. I was just really wild. I was a headache
for a few terms, grade one, I think, to grade five.
Then I went to another school and I settled down.
When I got away from Dad.

Mental Toughness and Motivation

P.K.:   For me, mental toughness is going to a ski hill and
running until you literally can't feel your legs anymore, and then, not only can you not run anymore
but you find the courage to look at your coach and
tell him that you want more, right? Mental toughness is when everybody else is quitting, or not everybody else can move forward, and you find a way.
When the going gets tough, I've always found a way
to get going and to elevate my game, or to elevate
my work ethic, or to do whatever I've had to do.
I don't know why that is.

            A lot is the environment you create around
yourself, the perception that your mind creates. For
me, the perception that my mind created is, "This
is the only way that I will be able to feed myself and
my family," or, "This is the only way I am going to be
able to help my family." So when I had to do an extra
rep, I didn't do it for myself. I did it because I wanted

to get to that level so I could dictate what type of life I was going to live. But that perception was not reality—me making it to the NHL was not going to determine whether we had food on our table or not. We always had food on our table. We always had clothes on our backs. We always lived in a nice house.

Racism and Criticism

P.K.:
I remember being upset [being called racist names as a child]. My parents took a very stern approach with me on that one. It was just, "You better get a whole lot tougher than that if you want to play in the NHL, if you want to compete." If you want to be somebody in this world, you need to find a way to turn the cheek on that. You'd better find a way to figure out how you're going to deal with that because that's going to come left, right, and centre. Even if it didn't come again, the mindset, coaching your mind on how to deal with things like that, was the point.

People don't understand. They attack the people that [made the racist comment]. No. You say to the person who's being attacked, "This is how you're going to deal with it, and I challenge you to deal with it like this every single time." Instead of feeling pity for yourself, you say, "I'm better than this. I'm above this. I'm not going to let anybody else dictate how I feel about it, or how I deal with it. That's what's going to happen."

I care about winning. I care about my team-mates, the guys who are going to help me win.

I care about the organization that pays me, that
pays my teammates, that helps us put food on our
families' tables. I care about my family. Those are
the people who actually have an influence on my
life. People who speak badly about me or take shots
at me, they don't have an influence on what I do
or how I feel in my life. The people who can help
me get to the goal that I want to get to, or who
can help my team get to the goal that we want to
get to—those are the people who I give a time and
place for, that's it.

The Family Today

P.K.:   I think we've all matured really well. It's great
          because we're able to establish our independence
          while still remaining a family. As everybody grows
          older, you find that's one of the toughest things to
          do, to keep your family together. I think we're in
          a great position—every summer we come back;
          we see each other a lot; we spend a lot of time as a
          family together. Every summer we have a barbecue
          where we invite all our family and friends, when we
          have our whole family there—nieces, nephews, the
          kids are in the pool. That is the best time for me.

Jordan: We're just a normal family. I think people always
          expect these great big things, but really we're just
          normal. I know it may sound kind of silly, having
          all three of us playing professional hockey and then
          saying that we're normal, but I'll say we're no differ-
          ent than the average family.

Acknowledgements

My first thank-you goes to my wife, Maria. Our goals in marriage were to have good jobs, good kids, a good home and a good life. These goals required teamwork to make them work and to make us work to our potential. I could not have found a better life mate. When I was lost Maria would lead the way. When life bent me like a tree in the wind she was the rod to make me straight again. When I had no energy, she was my inspiration. I could not have written this book without her encouragement, support and willingness to listen patiently while I read her pieces of my work. The first drafts are always rough around the edges but she never declined to listen. While she was always straightforward with her remarks, like a good teacher she never forgot to add encouragement along with her suggestions.

After Maria, my deepest gratitude goes to my five children. Raising them was a much bigger job than I ever imagined. All I wanted for each of them was to find that thing very early on they loved to do and to do it to the best of their abilities. They did that and much, much more. I like the fact they embraced that philosophy and were always willing to pay the price for what they ordered in life. It is their potential that we worked on growing that has driven me to write this book. In a way, they have given me exactly what I wanted to give them as a parent: a life, drive, passion, a dream, and things I love to do. Thanks to all of them for inspiring me to be the best parent I am capable of being, even though I wasn't always perfect.

Next in line for a thank-you are my mother, Fay, and father, Sylvester. My parents taught me how to love through the love they gave me. They taught me how to work hard through their own life achievements. They taught me how to live with others through their social network of friends from all walks of life. They started our family in Jamaica then migrated to Canada to start all over again. Both were approaching thirty years of age when they came to Canada but took on the challenges with the strength, patience and determination of Olympic athletes. They will always be my champions.

My dream during my adolescent years was to be a professional basketball player. That dream took me to Lakehead University in Thunder Bay where I made an impression on young Scott Colby, a student-athlete in a Thunder Bay high school. My relationship with Scott started in the gym with a ball but extended to the A&P grocery store on River Street where we both worked on evenings and weekends. It was basketball and groceries that connected us twenty-nine years ago and now it is the Team Subban story that is connecting us again in the form of a book that he is co-authoring with me.

Scott and I reconnected through an interview I did with his colleagues from the *Toronto Star*. When he told me that he wanted to add the word author to his resumé, it was easy for me say, "Let's do it." We had formed a relationship that was the source of our bonding that time did not erode. Scott, thanks for pushing, guiding, supporting and coaching me because I learned that I am capable of so much more working with you to write our book. Your tips were exactly what I needed, not just to write this book, but to tell a story that would be a difference maker to whoever cared to listen to my message, both personally and professionally.

Working with children has been my calling. I have worked with thousands of young people from the academic to the athletic domain. All I have always wanted to do for them was to help them to do better and be better, as students, athletes, and young people. I never lost faith in them no matter how they performed or behaved. I believe if they have an innate desire to do better it will eventually be realized. This book is about them too. When my students frustrated me, it pushed me to be better. When progress was difficult to see, I learned to remain hopeful. When it seemed they couldn't do right, I never lost sight of what was right about them, which is the beauty that they all possess inside. Thanks to the boys and girls for making me better. You are in the words, thoughts and stories found on the pages in this book.

Carolyn Forde, literary agent and international rights director at Westwood Creative Artists, planted our book idea and potential in the gardens of major publishing companies in Canada. Her knowledge, skills and belief in our project were the ingredients that have worked to give us a bountiful harvest: a book with Random House Canada. Thank you, Carolyn, for your leadership, coaching and direction. You have taken us further than I could have imagined.

Pamela Murray, senior editor, Random House Canada, thanks for believing in us, the story and opening a whole new world for me: authoring a book. I will never forget the first conversation we ever had. I shared hockey stories, school stories, parenting stories and life stories not knowing that I would have the pleasure of working together with you one day to fulfill my dream of writing and publishing a book. It takes many hands working together to place a book on shelves and your fingerprints are all over the pages of *How We Did It,* from the front cover to the back. Your insights and feedback were invaluable to us. They were relevant, pointed and were always made with the reader in mind, as well as maintaining the integrity of our story. We could not have done it without you, Pamela.

I am particularly grateful to a group of friends and colleagues whom I have interacted with over the years: Martin Ross, Dennis Boyce, Ken Boyce and Ron Kellman. They did not always know when they were part of my writing process. For example, I would parachute an anecdote, story or quote from my book into our conversation and would pay attention to their reactions. (Eventually I did reveal my motivations.) Their responses and feedback were invaluable.

I am also grateful to teacher Devon Jones, director of YACCE (Youth Associated for Achievement Academics Athletics and Character Education), who printed the "My Potential" verse on his staff uniform and T-shirts for their summer school students. Thanks, Devon, for recognizing the power in those words.

I have worked with many school leaders, from teachers to vice principals, principals, supervisory officers, and parents over my twenty-nine years in various school communities in the TDSB. There are too many names to mention on this page, but, I want to say thank you to all of them for making me better.

I have had many helpful conversations with my friend, Jim Watt. Jim, I am very grateful for your mentoring, coaching and friendship. Your influences on me are in my book.

Don Norman convinced me to make the backyard rink and shared his recipe for it. If I had not built that rink every winter for approximately fifteen years, there probably would be no book. Harnessing those extra hours practising, training and playing gave life to my sons' dreams.

Kameron Brothers was P.K.'s first formal skills developmental coach. P.K. has worked with him starting from around five years of age to the present day. He has had a lasting impact on P.K. the hockey player. Whatever I started with P.K., Kameron corrected what needed to be corrected and polished what needed to be polished. Thank you, Kameron.

— Karl Subban

A note from the co-author

I was present for the birth of Karl's dream to spend his life helping children develop their potential. In August of 1980 I was one of the first kids he coached at a Lakehead University summer basketball camp. The basketball community in Thunder Bay is small and the Lakehead players were our heroes. Karl, however, stood out from the rest of the camp's coaches. He had a way of drawing kids in and making them feel they mattered. And then there was Karl's work ethic, which was something to behold. No one worked harder on the court, or with the kids, than Karl Subban.

Over the next few years I would cross paths with Karl periodically. When I turned sixteen in the fall of 1981, I got a job bagging groceries and stocking shelves at the local A&P. Karl also worked there and I was honoured when he would occasionally ask me to punch his time card on Saturday nights so he could duck out fifteen minutes early to catch the hourly bus. (This was before he had purchased the legendary Betsy from a Thunder Bay Toyota dealership.)

My favourite experience with Karl came in the summer of 1982 when I was allowed to join a summer basketball league at Lakehead for senior high school and university players. I was placed on the same team as Karl, our captain and coach. Karl was no longer just a basketball mentor, he was my teammate!

In 1984, I graduated from high school and lost touch with Karl. But in the summer of 2013, when I was writing a parenting column for the Toronto *Star*, the universe conspired to make us teammates again. Out of the blue I received an email from a publicist wondering if I wanted to interview an NHL hockey dad about his charitable work helping underprivileged kids play hockey. I leapt at the chance to reconnect with Karl Subban and I wrote a column about him. The next step was obvious to me. Karl needed to write a book about his life—and I had to be the one to help him. So my biggest thank-you has to go to Karl for agreeing to embark on this special partnership and trusting me to help him tell his story.

I must also thank his entire family—Maria, Taz, Tasha, P.K., Malcolm and Jordan—for their co-operation and support throughout the project. It has been an honour getting to know all the members of Team Subban.

Special thanks also to coaches Harry Evans and George Burnett, for their time and their honesty, and to Chris Junghans of the Nashville Predators.

When I first met with Karl to discuss this project, I said that in order for this book to work he must be open with his readers and discuss mistakes he made along the way. Karl insisted he wouldn't have it any other way. To that point, I need to stress that during the interviews I did with Karl's family and with coaches Evans and Burnett, Karl was not present and set no restrictions. Everyone was encouraged to speak freely.

On the Team Colby side, I received tremendous support and encouragement from my parents, Dorothy and Peter Colby, and my brothers, Jim and Craig, and their wives, Lynn and Nancy, and my mother-in-law and father-in-law, Vera and Kersi Mistry.

I would not have reconnected with Karl if I had not been writing the column, so thanks to Janet Hurley at the *Toronto Star* for giving me the column and to Tania Pereira for taking such great care editing it.

Working on my first book was an intimidating prospect and I relied on fellow writers for advice and support. A well-deserved thank-you to Brett Popplewell, Peter Edwards, Marina Jimenez, Dan Robson, Bill Bishop and Antanas Sileika.

One writer in particular needs to be singled out, however, and that is Charlie Wilkins. Charlie has been a writing mentor to me since 1990 and it is not an exaggeration to say this book would not have been published with my name on the cover without his sage advice and guidance. I don't have enough space to outline all he has done for me, so he'll have to settle with a deep, appreciative thank-you.

One favour that Charlie did was to hook Karl and me up with his literary agency, Westwood Creative Artists, where we met our agent, Carolyn Forde. Carolyn was there from the infancy of this book, and as Karl described, her talent and belief in the project helped make this book a reality. What a great person to have in our corner. Thank you, Carolyn.

Karl and I were blessed to sign with Random House Canada. Senior editor Pamela Murray was the perfect fit and had an unrivalled passion for this book. Pamela was a joy to work with and her insightful edits, steady guidance and professionalism took this book to a higher level than we could have ever reached without her. Thank you, Pamela. I hope we are able to work together again.

If it takes a village to raise a child, it takes a small army to publish a book. Karl and I have deep appreciation for all the talented people with Team Penguin Random House Canada who made this book possible. They include, from the executive and publishing side: Brad Martin, Kristin Cochrane, Robert Wheaton, Anne Collins, Marion Garner, Barry Gallant, Scott Sellers, Deirdre Molina, Sarah Jackson and Liz Lee. From the sales team: Matthew Sibiga, Mary Giuliano, Jennifer Herman, Liza Morrison, Léonicka Valcius and Mike Rose. From marketing and publicity: Beth Lockley, Tracey Turriff, Jessica Scott, Lindsey Reeder, Ruta Liormonas and Jackie Cunningham. From production: Janine Laporte, Carla Kean and Brittany Larkin.

Credit for the elegant design of the book belongs to Lisa Jager. And thanks also to freelance editors Linda Pruessen, Doris Cowan and Noeline Bridge.

Karl and I need to thank Flammarion Québec for publishing the French translation of *How We Did It* and allowing this book to reach a wider readership in Quebec, where fans have been so important to this story and to Team Subban.

Karl and I also need to acknowledge high school student Jennifer Tran, whose moving poem arrived as we were working on revisions to the last chapter. It was an unexpected gift that seemed to have been written specifically for our book: #serendipity. Please continue writing, Jennifer.

Lastly, I must publicly acknowledge the support, understanding and patience of my wife, Natasha. She was on board from the beginning. In fact, she insists the book was her idea. Natasha made countless sacrifices over the years so I could squeeze in the time for interviews, writing and revisions. I will never be able to thank her enough, but I'll try. Thank you, Natasha. My twin children, Popcorn and Sweet Pea, were also inspirations to me and had to spend many days not seeing their dad while I conducted interviews and wrote. Thank you both, and I hope we have already started loading your GPS for success—Uncle Karl has set a high bar for Team Colby. And as Karl says, "The bar you set is the bar you achieve."

— Scott Colby

INDEX

KARL SUBBAN retired in 2013 after thirty years as a school teacher and administrator with the Toronto District School Board. He has worked with Canadian Tire on a project that teaches Canadian families about the important benefits of their children participating in hockey, and served as an ambassador for Hyundai Hockey Helpers Program. When Karl is not delivering empowering speeches to Canadian audiences on how to find one's potential, he spends time teaching his grandchildren how to skate.

SCOTT COLBY is the Opinions editor at the *Toronto Star* and a freelance writer.